Quilted Gardens

Floral Quilts of the Nineteenth Century

Quilted Gardens

Floral Quilts of the Nineteenth Century

Ricky Clark

RUTLEDGE HILL PRESS
Nashville, Tennessee

Published in Nashville, Tennessee, by Rutledge Hill Press, Inc., 211 Seventh Avenue North, Nashville, Tennessee 37219. Distributed in Canada by H. B. Fenn & Company, Ltd., 1090 Lorimar Drive, Mississauga, Ontario L5S 1R7.

Typography by D&T/Bailey Typesetting, Inc., Nashville, Tennessee
Design by Harriette Bateman

Library of Congress Cataloging-in-Publication Data
Clark, Ricky.
    Quilted gardens : floral quilts of the nineteenth century / Ricky Clark.
      p.   cm.
    Includes bibliographical references and index.
    ISBN 1-55853-272-2
    1. Quilting—United States—History—19th century. 2. Quilts—United States—History—19th century. 3. Quiltmakers—United States—History—19th century. 4. Flowers in art. I. Title.
    TT835.C56 1994
    746.9'7'097309034—dc20   94-2444
    CIP

Printed in Hong Kong
1 2 3 4 5 6 7 8—99 98 97 96 95 94

To Virginia Gunn, Ellice Ronsheim,
and Bari Stith
Good friends and inspiring teachers

Contents

Preface

It was a beautiful day in April 1988 when I returned to Austinburg. This little village, with its Greek Revival farmhouses and slate gravestones, was one of the earliest in Ohio. It had been our first home after leaving school; our children were born here. I loved the little town and its people.

This visit, however, was not entirely social. I was here to work at a quilt documentation day for the Ohio Quilt Research Project. When I entered the gymnasium set aside for our use, the first quilt was already hanging, ready to be photographed. It was gorgeous. A border of red flowers and green leaves surrounded four huge pots of full-blown and budding blossoms against a white background. What a way to begin a quilt day!

Three years later we included this quilted garden in the Ohio Quilt Research Project's book and exhibition, *Quilts in Community: Ohio's Traditions*. It was a beautiful example of an important style, the earliest embraced by quiltmakers everywhere in our state. I call this the classic floral quilt style.

Nineteenth-century floral quilts fascinated me then and continue to do so. They are undeniably attractive and eye-catching. As increasing numbers of them surfaced when I was working with the Ohio Quilt Research Project, they raised many questions in my mind.

Why was the subject matter in these quilts so uniform and the color scheme so specific? Why did nearly identical patterns recur so often? How did those patterns spread? When this style was popular, patterns for appliquéd quilts were not commercially available, yet apparently identical examples are found hundreds of miles apart. Or are they identical?

Why were these quilts popular in such a wide geographic area for so long? This was not a passing fad, found throughout the country for a year or two and then declared passé, only to be replaced by another. Classic floral quilts were immensely popular for approximately forty years, from the 1840s through the 1870s, with the style declining gradually thereafter.

Research in Ohio and Kansas indicates that many floral appliqué quilts were made by women of Germanic background. In Ohio these quiltmakers constituted an exceptionally large percentage in relation to the state's quiltmaking population as a whole. Why did these women find the style so appealing?

We addressed some of these questions in *Quilts in Community*, yet others still haunted me, and I was determined to find answers. My research took me far beyond the quilts and their makers, as I investigated complex social and economic factors that might have affected the style and pattern transmission of these lovely quilts during the mid-nineteenth century. I read descriptions of America written by early settlers and European visitors, articles from nineteenth-century newspapers, letters and diaries, and advice published in women's magazines. I explored the history of ornament, interior decoration, gardening, American agriculture, and technology. It has been an exciting quest.

In some respects, my terms are somewhat arbitrary. The quilt style I call "classic floral" is composed of identically sized blocks, usually in a repeated pattern. I have not included quilts with a single central focal point (the center medallion style), although some would otherwise fit my definition of classic floral quilts. I have organized the quilts according to their dominant structure within the quilt block and have named these structural categories myself after discovering that earlier sources are inconsistent in their nomenclature. Quilt pattern names are those used by the makers, when known; otherwise, by the owners. When no pattern names were reported, I have used names found in Barbara Brackman's *Encyclopedia of Pieced Quilt Patterns* and her *Encyclopedia of Appliqué*. In some cap-

tions a quiltmaker's married name is enclosed in parentheses, indicating that she made this quilt before her marriage. Both maiden and married names are included in the index.

In the first chapter I discuss the characteristic maker of classic floral quilts and the rapidly changing world in which she lived. The next chapter deals with earlier quilts that influenced the classic floral style and regional variations of that style. In "Roses or Carnations" I analyze the quilt patterns, organized by structure. This chapter includes only classic floral quilts made in Ohio. I invite researchers to compare these quilts with those in their own states, in hopes of building on my research and providing useful comparisons of structure or pattern. "Design Influences and Shared Style" addresses a variety of factors I believe influenced the development of the classic floral style, including other contemporaneous objects that share that style. Finally, in "Spreading the Word" I discuss two significant ways in which this quilt style was disseminated: agricultural fairs and westward migration.

My data include 179 Ohio-made classic floral quilts documented by the Ohio Quilt Research Project and independently by me, as well as examples published in sixty-three books, including state and re-

gional publications, museum catalogs, and quilt calendars. In addition, I contacted thirty-one museum curators and quilt researchers who were conducting surveys in twenty-four states between the East Coast and the Mississippi River, and others farther west, with specific questions about their findings. Most of these are members, as I am, of the American Quilt Study Group: Donna Bister, Hazel Carter, Katy Christopherson, Rita Erickson, Sue Hannan, Martha Ginn, Bettina Havig, Patricia Herr, Denise Hordberg, Laurel Horton, Cheryl Kennedy, Erma Kirkpatrick, Jeannette Lasansky, Marilyn Lemmon, Marsha MacDowell, Kathleen McLary, Margaret Ordoñez, Wendy Reed, Nancy Roan, Sandra Todaro, and Shelly Zegart. Special thanks go to Barbara Brackman, Mary Cross, Nancy Hornback, Jeana Kimball, Mary Lohrenz, Bets Ramsey, Jane Reeves, Phyllis Tepper, and Nancy Tuckhorn, who responded not only with answers to my questions but also with photos and documentation records of relevant quilts.

I owe much to librarians and archivists throughout the country, especially those at the Garden Center of Greater Cleveland, the Kansas State Historical Society, the National Agricultural Library, the Oberlin College Library, the Pennsylvania Horticultural Society Library, the University of Akron, the University of Delaware, and the Western Reserve Historical Society Library.

Staff members of many museums were extraordinarily helpful, including those at the Allen County (Ohio) Historical Society, the Clinton County (Ohio) Historical Society, the College of Wooster Art Museum, the Follett House Museum, the Rothman Gallery of Franklin and Marshall College, the Licking County (Ohio) Historical Society, the Lorain County (Ohio) Historical Society, the Ohio Historical Society, the Smithsonian Institution, the Stark County (Ohio) Historical Society, the Summit County (Ohio) Historical Society, the Valentine Museum, and the Western Reserve Historical Society. Darwin Bearley,

Cyril Nelson, Joel Kopp, and Tom Cuff were all helpful in my efforts to trace quilts with little recorded history.

Other quilt-loving friends helped in countless ways. Anita Reichard translated German documents for me. Carol Cleaves organized a team of helpers at the photo session to facilitate the work of photographer Tom Reed of KS Studios, Inc., including Diane Hienton, Lee Sigrist, Irene and Al Goodrich, Ellice Ronsheim, Kaye Schneider, and Harry and Ann Abbott. Botanizers Merry Jo Bailey, Virginia Gunn, Laurel Horton, and Ellice Ronsheim grew vintage prince's feathers to see if they look like the quilted versions. Marilyn Lemmon, Daphne Ginnings, and Jane Reeves helped me locate several wonderful quilts.

The owners of the quilts included here were most generous in allowing me to include their treasures and in providing information on the quiltmakers. They are to be commended for selecting such gifted ancestors.

I am especially grateful to my friends Patricia Cunningham, Virginia Gunn, Bari Oyler Stith, and Ellice Ronsheim, who have encouraged and supported me in this and earlier projects and who read the manuscript and provided helpful criticism. It is a pleasure to be working once again with the staff of Rutledge Hill Press, especially my editor, Ron Pitkin.

Finally, my deepest gratitude goes to my husband, David, for his unceasing encouragement, support, and patience with my obsessive enthusiasm for quilt history.

Quilted Gardens

Floral Quilts of the Nineteenth Century

1. Mexican Rose, 1868. Mary Ann Gonter (Shutt) (1852–1912). Baltic (Holmes County), Ohio. Floral Star structure, straight set, appliquéd, pieced, stuffed. Cotton. Signed and dated in embroidery. *79" x 77".* Collection of Martha Junkin.

Mary Ann Gonter was sixteen years old when she made this quilt in 1868, the year she married George Henry Shutt. It is inscribed "made in 1868 by M.A.G." in red embroidery.

Classic Floral Quilts

The Makers and Their World

2. Mary Ann Gonter Shutt

Sixteen-year-old Mary Ann Gonter was an accomplished seamstress by the time she made a Mexican Rose quilt to celebrate her wedding to George Henry Shutt in 1868 (see illustration 1). Her quilt is in a style with enduring appeal, which I call the classic floral style. Originating in the eastern United States during the 1830s, this style spread westward and remained a favorite in the settled regions of the country for approximately forty years, declining gradually during the rest of the nineteenth century. In terms of longevity and geographic spread, it was one of the most popular styles of the nineteenth century.

Quilts like Gonter's share a number of characteristics: a predominantly red and green color scheme on a white ground,[1] repeated blocks surrounded by a related border, conventionalized botanical mo-

tifs, and a red or green binding. They were made of cotton, even when silk, wool, and velvet quilts became popular. Most classic floral quilts are appliquéd. Often they are technically superb and, like Gonter's, may include stuffed work. Many are signed or dated; Gonter's is inscribed "made in 1868 by M.A.G."

Despite the consistent color scheme, subject matter, and organization of design elements, there are countless variations and subtle differences from one quilt to another. Quiltmakers selected different motifs to incorporate into their designs or combined them in different ways. They repeated them in four, nine, or twelve blocks and surrounded them with plain, pieced, or appliquéd borders of various designs. Occasionally blue replaces green in the color scheme, although in many cases this hue was originally green, created by overdyeing indigo with yellow, or vice versa.[2]

Mary Ann Gonter was born in 1852 in Baltic, Ohio, a town situated at the intersection of Tuscarawas, Holmes, and Coschocton counties. Her father, Elias Gonter, was a farmer. In 1860 he owned real estate valued at $5,500. Mary Ann's husband, George Shutt, was also a farmer, as well as a carpenter and cabinetmaker. Both Mary Ann and her husband were Germanic Protestants. George had helped build the Brethren Church in Baltic, of which they were members. After their wedding, Mary Ann and George bought a farm in Shanesville (now Sugar Creek), which remained in the family for three generations.

Mary Ann Gonter was characteristic of makers of classic floral quilts in the period 1840–1870, the golden age of this quilt style. A representative quiltmaker was a young woman with expert needlework skills who could afford to purchase fabric for her quilt. She might have made it for her wedding,

as in this case, or to commemorate some other special occasion. She would have lived in a settled, rural environment and the significant men in her life would have been farmers or skilled craftsmen and property owners. The quiltmaker's parents or grandparents were probably born in the eastern United States or were European immigrants, most likely from Germany. Her religious affiliation was Protestant.

This profile reflects the broader environment in which classic floral quilts were created: agricultural, but post-frontier; technologically advanced, yet still retaining hand skills. The world that produced classic floral quilts was neatly summarized in the corner blocks of a group of coverlets commercially woven in New York's Hudson River Valley between 1823 and 1834: "Agriculture and Manufactures Are the Foundation of our Independence."[3]

Agriculture

New York's coverlet weavers were not the first to document the importance of agriculture for America. As Benjamin Franklin noted in the late 1780s, "The great Business of the Continent is Agriculture. For one Artisan, or Merchant, I suppose, we have at least 100 Farmers, by far the greatest part Cultivators of their own fertile Lands." Throughout most of the nineteenth century, agriculture con-

3. Detail, Jacquard Coverlet
New York, 1830
The Ohio Historical Society

4. *The Ohio Cultivator,* 1856
Oberlin College Library

5. *American Country Life: Summer's Evening*
Lithograph published by Currier & Ives, New York, 1855
The Library of Congress

tinued as America's primary business.[4]

And America was expanding. Impelled by opportunities to own inexpensive land and to refashion it as the New Eden, one-quarter-million Americans moved west between 1840 and 1870.

"An Earthly Paradise"

From the earliest days of settlement, Americans believed they had a divine mission to civilize the wilderness, to transform the "unknown bounds of North America" into the New Eden. Based on a centuries-old

European vision, the "myth of the garden," as one historian has termed it, was to become an enduring cultural symbol of America, embracing a wealth of ideas: the ideal society was an agrarian democracy, its hero the independent, self-reliant farmer; farming was not only an occu-

❧ O! my dear mother . . . how every thought and recollection of my home came upon me I thought of the time when I was there and could associate with you — when you could come to our house and enjoy the blessed sweets of each other's company . . . I likewise thought of that cruel and hard heart I had thus to part with my friends — O! that parting moment when I was seated in the waggon [sic] to take (perhaps) a final farewell of all this world holds dear to me when I bid Grandmother farewell as she stood with weeping eyes to take her last look & I turned my back upon them . . . no mortal tongue can express my feeling at that time how I catched the last glimmer of the Dear old habitation — the fields the trees & everything else seemed to wear a gloomy aspect at my departure was the ways of heaven ever more dark than in my leaving you.

Laura Down Clark
Wakeman (Huron County),
Ohio 1818

pation, but a virtue; this agricultural society would expand westward indefinitely, situated in a "middle landscape" between the untamed, "howling wilderness" and the socially stratified, corrupt city.[5]

Although their terminology was identical, women and men probably perceived their roles in creating the New Eden differently. For men, access to affordable land and the vision of taming the wilderness "whose uncultivated forests and fertile plains, invited the uplifted *ax* and the furrowing *plough*" inspired westward migration. For most women, on the other hand, leaving their established homes was traumatic, as it involved the severing of cherished family ties. Their longed-for Eden was domestic, a home on the prairie "with a garden and flowers and creeping vines, and children and husband dear all at home, no more to roam."[6]

This *perceived* reality was fostered by promotional emigration literature, domestic fiction, and the popular lithographs of Currier and Ives. That it differed from the *factual* reality of rural western life, humorously described by a rural poetess (see page 8), in no way

negates it. For both women and men the pastoral myth, composed of shared iconography, ideas, and feelings, served to bind together a rapidly changing nation. It explained and reconciled many contradictory experiences of its citizens who admired individualism yet longed for community, who valued civilization yet confronted wilderness, who deplored the filth of the factory yet needed its products.

Life on the frontier was exhausting, rugged, dirty, and isolated. Classic floral quilts were not the product of the frontier but were made primarily in established rural communities. Decorated as most were with appliquéd designs and elaborate handwork, they were luxury items made by women who could devote considerable time to their fabrication.[7] Frontier life did not afford the leisure required to create such labor-intensive quilts. Furthermore, although they were handmade, classic floral quilts could not have been made much earlier than 1820 because their production depended on technological developments in a number of fields, especially textile production, transportation, and printing.

The Farmer's Wife

O! Tell me not of purling brooks,
  Or blossoms on the green spray nodding;
I think of all life's hooks and crooks,
  Of washing days and ceaseless plodding.
O! tell me not of shady bowers —
  The song of birds, the hum of bees,
The soft delights of rural hours,
  The husbandman's long days of ease —

When soars the gleesome lark on high,
  His anthem to the morn beginning,
My cheese must fill the press, or I
  Must set the big round wheel a-spinning.

And should my spirit feel the glow
  Of Poesy within it burning,
Must I from Mount Parnassus' brow
  Descend in haste — to do a churning!

Come, Cits, and listen to the cry
  Of bleating sheep, in wood and clearing:
You hear their music, but I sigh —
  Alas! the three long weeks of shearing.

Though like to Araby, the blest,
  The odors sweet of tufted clover,
I wish, with bones that ache for rest,
  This weary haying month was over.

Ye gay belles, caged, where leafy screens
  Scarce dot the walks, like ovens glowing;
Whose bosoms leap at sylvan scenes,
  A rainbow halo o'er them throwing.

Ye anglers in Dame Fortune's tide!
  Leave town — but not for baiting fishes;
Haste to my kitchen — bend your pride,
  And help me wash a ton of dishes.

> Mrs. J.M.M.
> *The Ohio Cultivator*
> September 1, 1859

Manufacture

The first such developments were improvements in textile technology. Until the early nineteenth century, materials for making quilts were either home-produced, therefore time-consuming, or imported, therefore expensive. However, rapid advances in both cotton manufacturing and textile printing during the first half of the century created more fabric at lower prices.

America's first cotton spinning mill began operation in 1793 and the first power loom in 1815. Both provided quiltmakers with inexpensive white fabric for the backgrounds of their quilts. Sewing thread, a material we take for granted today, was handspun from homegrown flax or cotton until the mass production of three-ply cotton sewing thread after 1801, providing quiltmakers with an economical means of decorative quilting. The development of cylinder printing in the 1820s expanded the amount of patterned fabric available and greatly reduced its cost. This printing technique, which used metal rollers instead of blocks or plates, allowed the continuous printing of designs on fabric, greatly hastening the printing process. By the 1830s, most women in settled areas could afford to purchase fabric for their quilts.[8]

These technological developments were concentrated in Europe and in America's eastern textile mills. However, fabric had to get to the consumers, not all of whom lived on the East Coast. By 1840, improvements in transportation opened some western regions to eastern markets, increasing access to materials and markedly reducing transportation costs. In Ohio alone those improvements were impressive.

The completion of New York's Erie Canal in 1825 immediately and dramatically affected Ohio's economy. Goods shipped overland from Philadelphia to Columbus in 1826 took thirty days. The same goods shipped from New York to Columbus via the Erie Canal took twenty days, at half the price. Pennsylvania and Ohio rapidly emulated New York's model. By 1845 Ohio had a complex canal system linking Lake Erie at Cleveland and Toledo to the Ohio River at Marietta, Portsmouth, and Cincinnati. This system, which included short feeder canals within the state and into Pennsylvania and Indiana, transported agricultural products to markets in New Orleans and on the East Coast, and brought cloth and other products from eastern manufacturers to Ohio.[9]

The related development of safe steamship travel further enhanced Ohio's economy, transporting both goods and

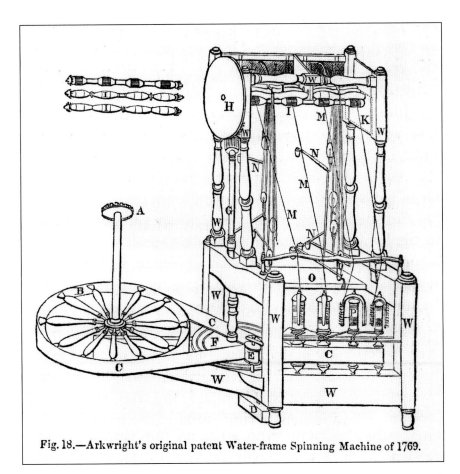

Fig. 18.—Arkwright's original patent Water-frame Spinning Machine of 1769.

6. Arkwright's original patent water-frame spinning machine of 1769
The Cotton Manufacture of Great Britain, Andrew Ure, 1836
Oberlin College Library

7. Broadside, Ohio

people into the state. Shipbuilding became a major industry on Ohio's northern and southern borders. Between 1811 and 1825 Cincinnati's boatyards launched twenty-six steamboats. Lake Erie's first steamboat, the *Walk-in-the-Water*, was built in 1818.

Overground travel also improved. The National Road, America's first east-west interstate highway, had reached Wheeling by 1817. By 1838 its Ohio link was completed, joining the cities of Cambridge, Zanesville, Columbus, and Springfield. It continued through Indianapolis and terminated in Vandalia, Illinois, in 1852. Railroads were also of increasing importance and eventually replaced canals. In 1850 Ohio operated 299 miles of railroad track. By 1860 the state had almost 3,000 miles, more than any other state, representing a tenfold increase in a decade.[10]

8. Walk-in-the-Water
History of the City of Cleveland, James
H. Kennedy, 1896
Oberlin College Library

THE HOUSE AND GARDEN.

This is a Monthly paper of 16 octavo pages, printed in superb style, and especially adapted to the interests of the House and Garden. The subjects embraced are: FRUITS, FLOWERS, VEGETABLES, RURAL ARCHITECTURE, INSECTS *injurious to the Orchard and Garden,* BEE-KEEPING *in all its departments,* POULTRY, PIGEONS, SINGING BIRDS, DOMESTIC RECIPES, &c. The volume commences with September.

TERMS:—Single subscribers, 50 cts. a year; four subscribers, $2, and one to the sender of the club; Clubs of ten, 45 cts. each; twenty, 40 cts. each; thirty, 35 cts. each; forty, 30 cts. each; fifty, 25 cts. each; and an extra number in each case to the getter up of the Club.

Teachers, Clergymen and Physicians are furnished at the lowest Club terms, or 25 cts. a year. Send for sample numbers, and get up a Club.

9. *The Ohio Farmer*, 1860
Oberlin College Library

Finally, improvements in printing technology brought newspapers, books, and magazines to more people faster and more inexpensively than ever before. How-to books were published in many fields, including home building, gardening, and household management. *Godey's Lady's Book* (1830), *Graham's Magazine* (1841), and *Peterson's Magazine* (1842) came into existence at this time. All included household and decorating advice directed toward women.

In settled areas, such technological developments signaled the closing of the frontier. In Ohio the pioneer period was over by 1840, except in the largely uninhabited northwestern corner of the state. Most residents now lived on established farms, in villages, or in cities. For the first time, quiltmakers in settled portions of America had more leisure for fancy needlework as the role of women gradually changed from producer to consumer.

❧ [A]griculture] is a business that God did not deem unworthy of himself—for he "planted a garden eastward of Eden."

A highly cultivated country, with its lawns, its parks and its flowers, speaks the religion of nature—the innate sentiments of the heart, which neither the primeval fall, nor the dark ages have been able to obliterate. We long for the lost garden of Eden before the bramble and the thistle usurped the place of the rose and the lily. This sentiment prompts us to combat with the elements—to struggle with the barren soil—to war with nature herself in order to realize the dreams of our race, which ever point to a lost Paradise. This strong affection for the beautiful landscape, the flowery mean, and tasteful gardens, is the harmonizer of our race.

It attaches man to some lovely spot, called HOME, where the affections of the heart are centered, and our household gods [sic] reside.

General Bierce
"An Essay Read at Medina, Ohio, September 15, 1853, at the County Fair"

10. The Nest at Home
Godey's Lady's Book, 1850
Oberlin College Library, Special Collections

"To Render Home a Paradise": Woman's Sphere

Closely related to the rapid developments in manufacture was the "cult of domesticity," a concept that emerged in eastern urban centers after the financial Panic of 1837, when men increasingly moved from farms to industrial cities to support their families and women's traditional handwork was supplanted by factory products. According to this concept, the lives of men and women became separated into gender-based "spheres," each with its assigned roles. While men embraced the world of commerce, women's sphere was domestic. "Home is woman's world; the training of the young her profession; the happiness of her household her riches; the improvement of morals her glory," as one influential editor opined.[11]

A woman was expected to instill high moral values in her husband and children by decorating her home with beautiful handwork. Home management included the cultivation of flowers, for "a woman never appears more truly in her sphere, than when she divides her time between her domestic avocations and the culture of flowers." Writers of advice books and magazines of the period described the ideal home as garden and sanctuary, Eden and heaven. These metaphors reflected women's socially prescribed domestic roles as nurturers and moral guardians. The interrelationship between women and gardening was further underscored by the botanical pen names used by several contemporary women writers: Fanny Forrester, Fanny Fern, Grace Greenwood, Minnie Myrtle, Lili Larkspur, Jenny June, and E.D.E.N. Southworth.[12]

Classic floral quilts emerged because of a confluence of factors: an established, post-frontier rural environment; improved transportation; and industrial developments in several fields, including textile technology and publishing.

Although less obvious, these quilts reflected two ideological concepts that were part of that same environment. One was the myth of the garden; the other, the cult of domesticity. Both stressed the importance of the garden and the home in women's lives. A more detailed examination of the impact of these concepts is included in "Design Influences and Shared Style."

Themes and Variations

Related Styles

Classic floral quilts were not without precedent. At least one-half century before the emergence of the classic style, American women created quilted gardens. It is not surprising to find that the earliest extant floral quilts were made in the Middle Atlantic States, former English colonies whose abundant natural beauty had long been extolled.

Forerunners of classic floral quilts are similar in design to medallion-style English and Welsh quilts made at the same time. Most have a central focal point surrounded by borders (see illustration 11). The floral motifs were printed on English chintzes, carefully cut along the edges of the printed designs and meticulously appliquéd to a white background, or composed from scraps or fabric pieces cut from larger motifs. Quiltmakers sometimes used strips of printed floral chintz as borders, and the quilting motifs were frequently botanical as well.

Because of the expense involved in purchasing imported fabric at that time, chintz appliqué quilts were largely associated with southern plantation aristocracy. The quilt in illustration 11 is attributed to the wife and daughter of Colonel Humphrey Hill of Hillsborough Plantation in Virginia, and young Frances Hill included several references to quilting in her 1797 journal. Chintz appliqué quilts remained popular in the Southern and Middle Atlantic coastal states into the early nineteenth century.[1]

During this same period, New England women also covered their beds with flowers. Early eighteenth-century counterpanes and woolen "bed ruggs," both imported and domestic, were embroidered in floral motifs. Later in the century New England needlewomen made or imported whole cloth quilts of calimanco, a glazed wool, on which they quilted elaborate floral designs

11. Chintz Appliqué Quilt, 1790–1820. Attributed to Frances Brook (Baylor) Hill (1748–1802) and Frances Baylor (Hill) Hill, Hillsborough Plantation (King and Queen County), Virginia. Appliquéd, stuffed. Cotton. 92" x 81". The Valentine Museum, gift of Mrs. Edward J. Mosley, Jr.

❧ All the Countries in the World, seated in or near the Latitude of *Virginia,* are esteem'd the Fruitfullest, and Pleasantest of all Clymates. . . . These are reckon'd the Gardens of the World.

Robert Beverley
The History and Present State of Virginia
1705

12. Calimanco Quilt, 1750–1800. Copp family, Stonington (New London County), Connecticut. Quilted. Wool. 100" x 92". National Museum of American History, The Smithsonian Institution, gift of John Brenton Copp.

similar to those they worked on quilted petticoats (see illustration 12). Like southern chintz appliqué quilts, New England calimanco quilts were in a medallion style.[2]

Although chintz appliqué and calimanco quilts were generated in discrete regions, by the second quarter of the nineteenth century the central medallion orientation was gradually replaced everywhere by identically sized blocks. This latter period saw the beginnings of the classic style of floral quilts.[3]

Regional Variations

Variations on this popular style existed in communities united by geographic, ethnic, or religious bonds. Probably the best-known regional style was made in Baltimore, Maryland, during the 1840s and 1850s (see illustration 13).

Baltimore quilts share several characteristics with those in the classic floral style: red and green color scheme, block and border structure, botanical motifs, cotton fabric, primarily appliqué technique. There are distinct differences, however.

First, many of the botanical motifs in Baltimore quilts are realistic, whereas those on classic florals are conventionalized. Second, rather than repeating one design in each block, Baltimore quiltmakers used a variety of designs. Third,

many Baltimore quilts were also album quilts, inscribed and signed like the autograph albums popular at the same time. In many cases, each block was signed with a different name, suggesting that groups of women made these quilts, with each woman selecting her own design. Differences in technical skill from one block to another support this thesis. In contrast, the classic floral quilt was usually the work of one quiltmaker.[4]

Because so many Baltimore quilts were group-made, designs are more varied than those on the classic floral style. A single quilt may include abstract shapes, pieced stars, buildings, trains, and monuments, as well as both conventionalized and realistic flowers. Indeed, many of the flowers and fruits in Baltimore's quilted gardens are recognizable and can be confidently identified as white and red roses, grapes, strawberries, and holly, because of the quiltmakers' careful selection of fabrics and use of ink or needlework. Some of the techniques used were layering, ruching (gathering), and embroidery to enhance details, or stuffing to create three-dimensional forms (see illustration 14).

Because of the detailed work involved in replicating specific flowers or buildings, these quilts were extremely labor intensive. Eleanor Sien-

13. Album Quilt, 1840. Mary Frances Whittington, Mary George, Baltimore (Baltimore County), Maryland. Diagonal set, appliquéd, stuffed, embroidered. Cotton. Signed and dated in ink. 112" x 107". Follett House Museum/Sandusky Library Association, gift of Mrs. William Sprow.

14. Detail of Illustration 13

15. Rose of Sharon, 1875–1900. Maker unknown, Brownstown (Lancaster County), Pennsylvania. Floral Star structure, straight set, appliquéd. Cotton. 78" x 80". Collection of Barbara J. Wamelink.

kiewicz, a contemporary quilt-maker who has reproduced Baltimore quilts and kept track of the time involved, estimates that it would take more than a year of forty-hour weeks to make a single quilt. Similar but less complex album quilts were made at the same time in near-by sections of Maryland, Pennsylvania, New Jersey, and New York.[5]

In contrast to the realistic designs found on many Baltimore quilts, the botanical devices on classic floral quilts are conventionalized: simplified, flat, and two-dimensional, yet still recognizably floral. They cannot confidently be identified as a particular flower but instead are generic. This is probably true even when we feel sure we recognize a specific blossom. The floral ornament today called coxcomb, for example, was seen by an art historian writing in 1892 as a pink, or carnation; motifs we now call tulips were identified as their relatives, lilies, by an antiquarian writing in 1948; and the pattern known in the South as Cotton Boll is the ancient Greek anthemion that decorates structures built in the fifth century B.C.[6]

Baltimore quilts were not the only regional variations of the classic floral style. The Heritage Quilt Project of New Jersey documented a few floral appliqué sampler quilts made between 1853 and 1867, all

from northern New Jersey. They also found repeated block classic floral quilts from the same time period, although most were pieced, rather than appliquéd.[7]

The New York Quilt Project found classic florals throughout the state and a few album quilts in this style made in New York's southeastern counties between 1845 and 1870.[8]

In the Germanic areas of southeastern Pennsylvania (northern Lancaster, Lebanon, and Berks counties), quilt-makers retained the conventionalized motifs and other characteristics of the classic style, but preferred an orange-yellow background. Researcher Patricia Herr reports finding equally as many classic floral quilts from this same region worked on a small blue and white printed background (see illustration 15). Both styles date from the 1860s or late 1850s. Polly Allison duPont notes "intense color" as a characteristic of quilts in Berks County, including several from the very late nineteenth and early twentieth centuries. By contrast, Jeannette Lasansky found only white backgrounds on the classic floral quilts she documented in central Pennsylvania, a region with fewer Germanic quiltmakers.[9]

Some North Carolina quiltmakers also selected a yellow background, which re-

16. Unnamed pattern, 1850–1900.
Nancy Stafford Spoon Shoffner
(1834–1906), Alamance County,
North Carolina. Symmetrical bouquet
structure, straight set, appliquéd,
pieced. Cotton. *74" x 88".* North
Carolina Quilt Project.

Nancy Spoon Shoffner was a trained
seamstress; early in her life she had
been apprenticed to a tailor. She made
both pieced and appliquéd quilts, including a second one in this pattern.

The St. Louis County Fair

All that ever makes a Floral Hall the great attraction, was there, even to the bed quilts, which seem ubiquitous, and the same great splotches of red and green stitched upon white, the same little bits of calico cut into squares and blocks; only that most of the display here was silk and satin, instead of calico, for our liberal gentlemen offered a premium of fifteen dollars on silk quilts. The one that took the premium was patched in squares of Job's troubles, (poor Job!—had he been given a choice to choose between such a quilt and his boils, he would have taken the boils,) set together with large squares of black satin, with a wreath of flowers or a boquet [sic] embroidered with silk upon every patch. Dear, oh dear! it would take more than one silver goblet to induce me to give a whole year to such a work.

Aunt Fanny
The Ohio Cultivator
October 1856

searchers in the North Carolina Quilt Project have dubbed "Alamance yellow" after the county where they discovered the most examples (see illustration 16). Many of these North Carolina women had ancestors in Pennsylvania.[10]

In all other states contacted, both northern and southern, westward to the Mississippi River, white was the preferred background color. Except in northern New England, where few classic floral quilts were reported, this was considered a significant style.[11]

Other Contemporaneous Styles

Other quilt styles, of course, coexisted with classic floral quilts, but few were as rigidly defined. For example, repeated block pieced quilts were popular during the same period. Some were fabricated in the popular red and green combinations, but quiltmakers used a wide range of patterns and other colors. Some of these styles can be identified with particular regions. In New England and western areas set-

tled by New Englanders, for instance, pieced quilts with structurally identical blocks and no borders were popular from the 1840s on. Another style, the trapunto sampler, was popular during this same period in Ohio, particularly in the southeastern counties.[12]

Later quilt styles, such as postage stamp, log cabin, and crazy quilts were more widely dispersed, named and explicitly described in farm journals and ladies' magazines, complete with instructions and patterns. Directions for making crazy quilts were first published in 1882. Only five years later the editor of *Godey's Lady's Book* decreed, "We regretted much the time and energy spent on the most childish, and unsatisfactory of all work done with the needle, 'crazy' patch-work." Quiltmakers were not deterred by the editor of *Godey's*, however, and continued to make crazy quilts and their successors, outline quilts, in what Virginia Gunn describes as "grass-roots responses" to the Aesthetic Movement in America.[13]

17. Abolitionist Quilt, 1842.
Members of the Hadley, McCracken, Bailey, Coate, Relles, Bangham, and Coggeshall families, Clinton County, Ohio, and Newport (Wayne County), Indiana. Sampler, diagonal set, appliquéd, pieced, embroidered. Cotton. Signed in ink. 72" x 72". Clinton County (Ohio) Historical Society.

The makers of this quilt were all members of the Religious Society of Friends (Quakers) and included Rebecca Hadley of Clinton County, Ohio, her daughters, and several other relatives. Some had joined a Quaker migration from Ohio to Newport (now Fountain City) in the 1820s. The Clinton County Friends' Meetings supported abolition, but

those in Newport were painfully divided over whether Friends should participate in illegal antislavery activities. Within a year of the making of this quilt, the Indiana women who participated left or were dismissed from the Indiana Yearly Meeting of Friends and joined other abolitionists in establishing the Indiana Yearly Meeting of Anti-Slavery Friends.

Roses or Carnations
The Quilt Patterns Analyzed

18. Rebecca Harvey Hadley (1795–1876), top, and Jonathan Hadley (1793–1879), bottom.

In view of the long and widespread popularity of classic floral quilts, it is surprising that the style is so rigid. This is the only style with a specific color scheme, the only one with uniform subject matter, and—except for the log cabin quilt—the only style with a consistent organization of design elements. Further, the quilt patterns are organized into a very few structures.

Within these strict guidelines, however, there is remarkable diversity. Flowers are usually viewed full face or in profile; however, they may be small or large, red or yellow, solid or delicate. Quiltmakers may emphasize the blossom at the end of a stem or an abstract design in the center of the block. Their patterns may be elaborate vases filled with bouquets or four leaves arranged in a simple cross. Red, green, or a third color may be emphasized.

As noted in the Preface, the quilts in this chapter were made by Ohio women. These and other Ohio classic floral quilts may therefore reveal an aesthetic different from those in other regions. For example, Ohio quiltmakers use both straight and diagonal sets. Sashwork is rare and, when used, is usually white. Many Ohio quilts from the 1850s and 1860s are dated in appliqué, quilting, or embroidery, although this was not a factor in selecting them for this book. So many in this and other styles include names and dates embroidered in red stem-stitch that I suspect these may be later additions by descendants of the makers. Although I did not pursue it as part of this project, it may be that in the 1890s there were published suggestions and instructions to record information about the makers of inherited quilts, just as so

many of us urge today's quiltmakers and quilt owners to
stitch documentary labels to the
backs of their quilts.

Finally, a favored quilting
pattern—especially in borders
—was units of from two to five
rows of closely spaced, parallel
diagonal lines, separated by an
inch or so of unquilted areas. I
hope readers will keep these
characteristics in mind and
compare this group of classic
floral quilts to those made in
their own states.

Because I analyze classic
floral quilts according to the
predominant structure of their
field patterns, a word about my
terminology is in order. I use
three terms in discussing these
structures: *motif, design,* and *pattern.* The motif is the basic design unit: blossom, bud, stem,
or leaf. Several motifs are combined to create a design: a plant
or floral branch, for example. A
design may be repeated and
two or more organized into a
pattern that fills a quilt block.
One pattern is usually repeated
in different blocks throughout
the quilt and is the source of the
name we use to describe it, such
as Rose of Sharon.

Set refers to the orientation
of the quilt blocks. In a straight
set the blocks are joined in horizontal rows. In a diagonal set
the rows are diagonal, hence
the blocks appear *on point,* another term for this arrangement. I refer to axes (vertical,
horizontal, diagonal) within the

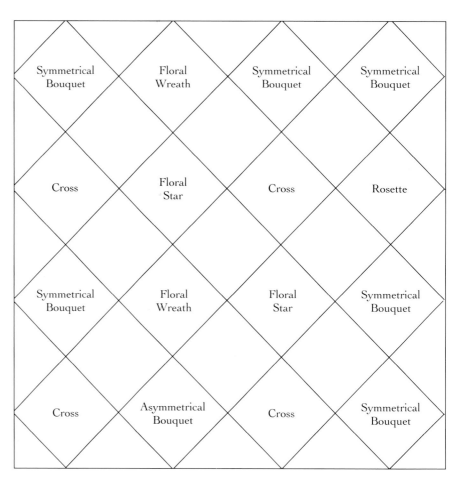

**19. Design structures used in the
Abolitionist Quilt, illustration 17**

quilt block. Formal structures of field patterns include Crosses, Floral Stars, Rosettes, Floral Wreaths, and Prince's Feathers; containers of flowers, including pots, baskets, and vestigial holders; and both symmetrical and asymmetrical sprigs or bouquets.

Crosses, Floral Stars, Rosettes, and Prince's Feathers are closely related, as each is based on the geometric division of the quilt block along regularly spaced axes and is radially symmetrical; the floral designs seem to grow, or radiate, from the center. These designs may be composed of straight or curved lines; their general direction is axial. While Floral Wreathes are circular, they often include blossoms placed along these same axes.

Containers of flowers and symmetrical sprigs or bouquets are bilaterally symmetrical, composed of a primary design unit flanked by a secondary element repeated in mirror image, one facing left, the other, right (dAb). Asymmetrical sprigs are not geometrically determined. All these structures are used in the unusual sampler quilt in illustrations 17 and 19.

Appliquéd borders include undulating vines, swags and tassels, pots of flowers (sometimes flanked by S-curves or vines), and birds. Borders may be pieced or made from plain fabric strips, both white and colored. Quilted designs in plain borders often include undulating vines or other designs also used in appliquéd borders. Each of these has a long history in the vocabulary of decorative arts and was readily available to nineteenth-century quiltmakers in architectural forms and home furnishings of the day.

Cross

The simplest of the radially symmetrical structures is the Cross, the scheme Barbara Hosler has used in her quilt (see illustration 21). In this structure the design units lie along the diagonal of the quilt block and radiate from the center, as indicated by the direction in which the leaves are growing. Hosler's pattern has only one design unit, repeated four times. Her coloring is unusual in that she uses green as a secondary color, appearing only in the vine.

20. Cross structure

The structure of Amanda Beem's quilt (illustration 23) might also be considered a

21. Laurel Leaves, 1852. Barbara
Hosler (d. c. 1853), Mount Blanchard
(Hancock County), Ohio. Cross
structure, straight set, appliquéd,
stuffed. Cotton. Signed and dated in
embroidered chain stitch. 83" x 73".
The Ohio Historical Society.

Barbara Hosler died a young woman
within a few years of completing this
quilt. All appliquéd units are stuffed
from the top of the quilt. All the fabrics used for appliqué are prints. In an
unusual variation, she uses pink and
blue as her primary colors and green
as a secondary color for the vine.

cross. The prominent designs appear vertical and horizontal because Beem's quilt blocks are set on point, whereas Hosler's are arranged in a straight set. Unlike Hosler, Beem also has a central design, which she has emphasized by size and color.

Floral Star

Although Beem's compositional scheme is clearly related to the Cross, it might also be considered a Floral Star, because Beem has placed the tiny green leaves emerging from behind the central flower along the vertical and horizontal axes, a characteristic of the Floral Star structure. In this respect, the structure of Beem's pattern is identical to that in block a-2 in illustration 17.

22. Amanda Beem Rhodes.

23. Old Tulip, 1856. Amanda M. Beem (Rhodes) (1828–1912), New Albany (Franklin County), Ohio. Cross or Floral Star structure, diagonal set, appliquéd. Cotton. Signed and dated in quilting. 84" x 66". Collection of Ann Abbott.

Amanda Beem made this quilt in 1856, the year she married William Jackson Rhodes. Many years later she presented the quilt to her friend, Martha Taylor, in whose family it has descended. Amanda's father, John Beem, was a miller who had come to Ohio from Maryland in 1812. He married Margaret Alberry in 1818. Amanda was the third of their four children. Amanda and her husband had three children.

Both these quiltmakers were aware of the vertical/horizontal axes of their quilt blocks, although they chose to emphasize other units.

The Floral Star structure usually has three design elements: a central unit and two others, one repeated along the vertical and horizontal axes, the other along the diagonals. The diagonal axis, as the longest element, is automatically emphasized. The central unit is also important because of its location. Through strong color or massive shapes, or by minimizing one of these elements, as

Beem did, quiltmakers can further stress any of these units.

Martha Kennedy Reamer's quilt, also set on point, emphasizes the diagonal designs through size and units of solid color. However, her vertical/ horizontal units are more pronounced than Beem's. Not only are these units longer than those in Beem's quilt, but Reamer has increased their length slightly by curving the line. The delicacy of these units makes a pleasing contrast with the more solid central and diagonal units and relates nicely to the secondary circular pattern,

26. Currants and Coxcombs, 1875–1900. Martha Kennedy Reamer (1856–1933), West Township (Columbiana County), Ohio. Floral Star structure, diagonal set, appliquéd. Cotton. *76" x 76".* From a private collection.

Martha was the daughter of Rachel Martin and William Kennedy, a farmer and stone mason. Both her parents were immigrants, Rachel from Canada and William from Ireland. In 1883 Martha Kennedy married John Reamer, also a farmer. They had two children and raised a nephew as well. Martha's quilt originally had an additional border on two adjacent sides. Enough of these borders remain to indicate that the appliquéd pattern was an undulating vine with currants.

25. Martha Kennedy Reamer and daughter, Alvina Belle

24. Diagram of Floral Star structure

composed of the same dot motifs in alternating colors.

Like Reamer, Lydia Pancoast has chosen to emphasize the designs lying along the diagonal axes of her quilt blocks. Because her quilt is arranged in a straight set, however, these prominent designs create an X, rather than a cross, within each block (see illustration 27).

The undulating floral vine surrounding the blocks in these quilts is one of the most popular border designs in classic florals. They relate to the field patterns in color and subject matter and sometimes introduce new floral motifs.

The next quilt, while quite different from Pancoast's and Reamer's, is also an example of the Floral Star structure (see illustration 29). Eliza Mincks's central designs gain importance through size and strong color, as well as by their key placement in each block. The floral designs along the diagonals, although the longest units, are minimized by their delicate, thin stems and relatively small blossoms.

Mincks's quilt is particularly powerful because her field consists of only four blocks. This increases the size of the pattern and emphasizes the center of the quilt by creating a secondary pattern where the blocks join. Secondary patterns can occur at the intersections of adjacent blocks when there are more than four blocks in a quilt.

28. Lydia White Pancoast

27. Lydia's Quilt, 1850–1875. Lydia White Pancoast (1834–1894), Wayne Township (Belmont County), Ohio. Floral Star structure, straight set, appliquéd. Cotton. 93" x 91". From a private collection.

The green fabric in Lydia's Quilt is colored by an early dye method. Lydia White Pancoast was born in Belmont County, Ohio, as was her husband, William. They married in 1853. Both families had migrated from Virginia; Lydia was a descendant of John White, governor of Walter Raleigh's second colony in Virginia. Lydia and William had fourteen children, seven boys and seven girls.

29. Rose of Sharon with Cat, 1854. Eliza Mincks (b. 1821), Jackson Township (Noble County), Ohio. Floral Star structure, straight set, appliquéd. Cotton. Dated in appliqué. 82″ x 84″. Collection of Kathryn Bell.

Historians studying the lives of American women have focused on their letters and diaries as primary documents. This quilt is eloquent testimony that their handwork is also evidence for historical research; Eliza Mincks could neither read nor write. Another of her quilts, also dated in appliqué, survives. Eliza was born in Maryland in 1821. Her husband, Hiram, was a farmer born in Pennsylvania. They had eight children. In addition to quilting and raising children, Eliza worked as a domestic.

30. Rose and Feather, 1856. Mary Ann Kepler (Rininger) (1835–1926), Green Township (Summit County), Ohio. Rosette structure, straight set, appliquéd, pieced. Cotton. Dated in appliqué. *76" x 78".* Collection of Wilma L. Blankenship.

Green Township, Mary Ann Kepler Rininger's home, was a close-knit Germanic community settled in 1809 by migrants from Bucks and Centre counties in Pennsylvania. Mary Ann's grandfather was one of the town's earliest settlers. Mary Ann married William Rininger in 1867, and they raised two children. Her quilts reflect the love of bold colors associated with Germanic quiltmakers.

In a quadrant arrangement, however, this intersection occurs only once, always at the quilt's center.

The Floral Star is a popular structure. Many patterns in this category are known today by their rose-related names, as identified by Carrie Hall and Rose Kretsinger in their 1935 publication *The Romance of the Patchwork Quilt in America*: Mexican Rose, Ohio Rose, California Rose, and Rose of Sharon.

Rosette

Closely related to the Floral Star is the Rosette structure. Like the Floral Star, the Rosette is radially symmetrical, its design elements aligned along regularly spaced axes. The Rosette, however, has only two designs: a central unit and another radiating from it equal-

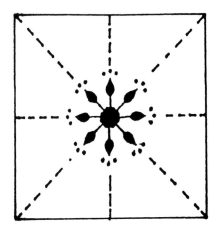

31. Rosette structure

ly along all axes. The resulting Rosette form is circular.

Mary Ann Rininger's quilt is bold because her buds are large and her central rosette complex, enclosing an eight-pointed star with a disc at the center (see illustration 30). This quilt is particularly exciting because the repeated rosettes establish secondary patterns where the blocks join. Rininger's unusual appliquéd bor-

32. Three generations of the Rininger family. *Left to right,* daughter Nora R. Killinger, granddaughter Elta R. Ries, daughter-in-law Laura R. Roush, quiltmaker Mary Ann Rininger, husband William Rininger, son-in-law Albert Killinger.

33. Great Grandma Stewart's Quilt, before 1878. Eliza Jane Duff Stewart (1786–1878), Knox Township (Guernsey County), Ohio. Rosette structure, straight set, appliquéd. Cotton. 96" x 77". Collection of Janet Patton Doyle.

This quilt has an unusual and apparently original border as well as sashwork, which is rare in Ohio quilts. Eliza's parents were of Scots-Irish descent. Her mother died when she was nine and she was raised by relatives. She married William Stewart and they had four children. Both her father and her husband were farmers. Eliza earned a degree in business, a fact she kept secret from her children. According to family tradition, she wanted to live to be ninety. She surpassed that goal by two years.

der is effectively set off from the field by the inner, pieced border.

The primary pattern in Eliza Stewart's quilt, while quite different from Rininger's, is still an example of the Rosette structure (see illustration 33). These Rosettes have an active, exciting effect on the viewer. When seen from a distance, they can be seen either as red flowers on a white ground or as a white eight-pointed star on a green-and-red ground. Because this is a change in our perception, rather than in the quilt itself, the image appears to shift before our eyes.

Stewart's secondary pattern is a Cross, with the central unit emphasized. These are placed at the intersection of sashes between the quilt blocks. Although sashwork is not uncommon in many areas of the country, it is unusual in Ohio, where this quilt was made.

Prince's Feather

The Prince's Feather (also called Princess Feather) and Rosette structures are related in that they have only two design units, with the second repeated along regularly spaced axes. There are enough distinctions, however, to consider Prince's Feather a separate category.

First, the repeated design is always a long, curved leaf that gives a sense of whirling motion to the pattern. Second, although in many Prince's Feather quilts this leaf is re-

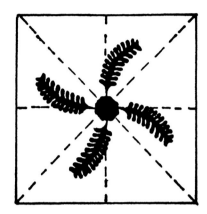

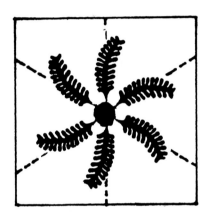

34. Prince's Feather structure

35. Prince's Feather, 1853. Keziah Redman (Burk) (1827–1910), Zoar (Tuscarawas County), Ohio. Prince's Feather structure, straight set, appliquéd. Inscribed and dated in quilting. Cotton. 82" x 82". Collection of the Western Reserve Historical Society, Cleveland.

When Keziah Redman made this quilt she was being courted by Thomas J. Williams, whose name and the date "1853" she quilted between two feathers in the lower right corner of the quilt. She was married a year later — to Hiram C. Burk. They had four children.

❧ I remember that [Grandfather] had allowed to remain among his turnips two or three plants, known to us as the Lady-fingers, which he carefully hoed along with his vegetables, evidently cherishing the common belief that the plant kept out weeds. This beautiful plant, with its slender jointed and collared stock, its gracefully poised, rather wide-spreading branches, with their pendant plumes of bright red, was often seen about the gardens and farmyards. It was sometimes called Kiss-me-over-the-fence, alluding to its habit of swaying in the least wind and touching you on the cheek as you went by. Its common bookname is Prince's Feather.

Irene Hardy
The Making of a Schoolmistress
1913

peated eight times, in others it occurs four or six times. Finally, most Prince's Feather quilts from Ohio have one or four blocks, rather than the nine or twelve usually found in Floral Stars and Rosettes.[1] A comparison of quilts in this category shows how diverse they can be, despite their similarities (see illustrations 35, 37, and 38).

Keziah Redman's Prince's Feather has eight leaves; Prudence Wells's, six; and Mary Ann Rininger's, four. Although the leaves in all these quilts have serrated edges, Redman's are so deeply incised that they look like leafy branches. The leaves of the prince's feather plant (*Amaranthus hypochondriacus*) are actually red and green, and the quiltmakers address this differently. Redman and Wells have alternated red and green solid-colored leaves, with Wells inserting floral units between her leaves; and Rininger has divided each leaf into two colors. Furthermore, each quiltmaker has used a different design in the center of her quilt

36. Keziah Redman Burk and daughter Cora

37. Prince's Feather, 1863. Prudence Wells (b. 1830), Wellston (Jackson County), Ohio. Prince's Feather structure, straight set, appliquéd. Cotton. Signed in embroidery. 81" x 80". The Ohio Historical Society.

According to family tradition, this quilt was in the frame in July 1863 when Confederate Col. John Morgan and his cavalry raided the Wellston area. Morgan's Raid was the only Civil War action within Ohio. Their pillage was "a mania; senseless and purposeless," according to Morgan's second in command. Among the items they stole were a birdcage with three canaries in it, seven pairs of skates, and bolts of calico. Most raiders discarded their plunder after a few days, "like children tired of their toys."

blocks, all of them also popular central units in Floral Star and Rosette quilts.

The borders of these quilts are different, although each quiltmaker has used a standard border design. Redman's blooming trees are unusual. Redman and Rininger have effectively related their borders to the field patterns by alternating red and green in the primary border motifs, Redman in her pots and Rininger in her swags. Rininger's swags also echo her curved, serrated leaf shapes. All three quiltmakers have introduced new motifs into their borders.

38. Prince's Feather, 1850–1875. Mary Ann Kepler Rininger (1835–1926), Green Township (Summit County), Ohio. Prince's Feather structure , straight set, appliquéd. Cotton. *76" x 76".* Collection of Wilma L. Blankenship.

This is the simplest form of the Prince's Feather. It is an old Germanic pattern, the whirling swastika. The blossoms hanging from the tassels are the same as Rininger used in her Rose and Feather quilt in Illustration 30.

39. Rose Wreath, c. 1844. Mary Nelson Nyman (1823–1905), Peru (Huron County), Ohio. Floral Wreath structure, straight set, appliquéd, stuffed. Cotton. Initialed in stuffed quilting. 96" x 82". Collection of Mary Laning Stewart.

Mary Nelson was the daughter of John and Almira Sherman Nelson. Her father, a farmer and millwright, was a pioneer settler of Peru, having come there from Massachusetts in 1816. Mary raised five younger siblings after her mother's death, and in 1844 she married Benjamin Nyman. She lived in an era of rapid change. In Peru Mary saw wheat wagons backed up seven miles en route to the canal in Milan, then the second largest grain port in the world, now a small village ten miles south of Lake Erie. She witnessed the end of the canal era there, when the railroads bypassed Milan and were routed through Norwalk. Her husband had invested in the railroads, and in 1875 the Nymans moved to Norwalk where Benjamin financed several business buildings. They had no children, but Mary Nyman was known as "good Aunt Mary to half the village of Peru."

Floral Wreath

The Floral Wreath is another popular structure. Despite the circular nature of this pattern, makers of Floral Wreath quilts frequently place floral motifs on the wreaths where they are intersected by the vertical, horizontal, or diagonal axes of the quilt block.

Mary Nelson Nyman has arranged four red flowers on the vertical and horizontal axes of the quilt block, then set sprouting floral buds along the diagonal axes (see illustration 39). She has alternated appliquéd blocks with plain ones and quilted floral wreaths identical to her appliquéd patterns in the plain blocks. Both her appliquéd and quilted wreaths are stuffed, as are her initials, quilted in the cartouche in the top border.

40. Floral Wreath structure

41. Single Rose, c. 1860. Julia Hayden Marshall (1815–1885) and Frances Marshall McClurg, Greer (Knox County), Ohio. Floral Wreath structure, straight set, appliquéd, reverse appliquéd, embroidered. Cotton. 86" x 82". The Ohio Historical Society.

Julia Marshall and her daughter Frances collaborated on at least two quilts. Julia came from Otsego, New York, where her parents had one of the first textile mills there. Julia's husband, Edward G. Marshall, was a coverlet weaver who worked in several woolen mills in eastern Ohio.

An unusual Floral Wreath quilt was made by Julia Hayden Marshall and her daughter, Frances (illustration 41). These squared wreaths are actually undulating vines bordering each of the four quilt blocks. The plain white border is also quilted in an undulating vine, and quilted roses fill each block.

Floral Vase

Floral Star, Rosette, and Prince's Feather structures are radially symmetrical. By contrast, the Floral Vase is bilaterally symmetrical and has a vertical orientation. Floral designs typically develop upward, as from a vase, urn, basket, or vestigial container.

Lucinda Painter's spectacular 1854 quilt in illustration 43 is an example of this compositional scheme. Her border design, a flower pot flanked by S-curves, was popular with many Ohio quiltmakers.

The quilt in illustration 44, made in Ohio circa 1860, is a simpler version of the Floral Vase structure. Although the maker's name is unknown, this quilt has much in common with two others made by Mary Ann Rininger of Summit County at about the same time. The maker's aesthetic preference for masses of color is similar to Rininger's, and the design of her unusual outer border is identical to that in Rininger's Rose and Feather quilt, even to the colors and size of each motif

42. Floral Vase structure

43. Flower Basket, 1854. Lucinda Painter (b. 1832), Pike Township (Stark County), Ohio. Floral Vase structure, straight set, appliquéd, stuffed, embroidered. Cotton. Signed and dated in embroidery. 82" x 90". From the collection of the Stark County Historical Society, Canton, Ohio.

Lucinda Painter was the oldest of ten children. Her parents, Joseph and Sarah Painter, were born in Pennsylvania, and her father was a farmer. In 1860 Lucinda was still living at home. All the berries on Lucinda's elaborate quilt are stuffed. She used a French curve to trace some of her quilting patterns.

44. Pot of Flowers, c. 1860. Maker unknown, Ohio. Floral Vase structure, straight set, appliquéd, pieced. Cotton. 78" x 78". America Hurrah Antiques, New York City.

This quilt is remarkably similar to Mary Ann Rininger's quilts in illustrations 30 and 38, including nearly identical size and similar borders. Not only is the design of the unusual outer border of this quilt the same as the one in Illustration 30, but the placement of colors in each motif is identical. The maker of this quilt must surely have seen Rininger's Rose and Feather quilt and had access to the templates, if the maker was not Rininger herself.

45. Tulip, 1846. Made by or for Mary Ogier, Clinton Township (Vinton County), Ohio. Symmetrical Bouquet structure, diagonal set, pieced, stuffed, appliquéd. Cotton. Signed and dated in stuffed quilting. 95" x 99". America Hurrah Antiques, New York City.

This quilt has much in common with a number of trapunto sampler quilts with similar borders made in southern and southeastern Ohio during the same period. When this quilt was purchased in southern Ohio, the only information about it was provided by the quiltmaker: the quilted and stuffed name *Mary Ogier* and the date *1846*. The 1850 census lists only two people of that name in southern Ohio, both living in Clinton Township, probably related. One was a fifty-five-year-old widow born in France and living with her four children and another young child, all born in Ohio. Her oldest son was a farmer and Mary was a property owner and head of household. The other Mary Ogier was a child born in 1844, the daughter of William and Ann Ogier, both thirty-two in 1850. William Ogier was a farmer and property owner originally from Pennsylvania. His wife was born in Maryland, and they had five children, also born in Ohio. It may be that Ann Ogier made this quilt for her daughter Mary.

within this design (see illustration 30). Because the dimensions of the two quilts are nearly identical and the number of border units the same in each, it appears that they were cut from the same template. Further, this quiltmaker's inner border is identical to the one Rininger chose for her Prince's Feather (illustration 38).

The preceding Floral Vase quilts are appliquéd. However, this category also includes pieced containers, such as baskets (see illustration 86) and vestigial containers, often triangular shapes. Stems, leaves, and flowers are typically appliquéd. In these patterns, the containers usually emerge from a corner of the quilt block. In order for the patterns to appear upright when viewed from the edges of the quilt, the blocks are usually set on point.

Symmetrical Bouquet

A related category is the symmetrical sprig or bouquet. Mary Ogier's quilt is one example (illustration 45). Like Mary Nyman, this quiltmaker has echoed her pattern in the plain blocks, first outlining them in quilting stitches, then stuffing them. Her spectacular quilting and stuffed work greatly enhance her simple pieced pattern. Several other versions of this structure can be seen in illustration 17.

46. Symmetrical Bouquet structure

47. Rose, 1858. Sarah Jane Beatty, Sarahsville (Noble County), Ohio. Asymmetrical Sprig and Floral Star structures, straight set, appliquéd, stuffed, embroidered. Signed and dated in embroidery. Cotton. 84" x 84". Collection of Jo Louise Brown.

The spectacular technique and lush nature of this asymmetrical pattern is refreshing. The quilting pattern in the border consists of four closely spaced rows of diagonal lines, separated by an inch of unquilted area. It is so closely quilted, with most quilting lines running in the same direction, that the quilt is difficult to hang straight. Little is known about the quiltmaker, but this was one of a number of quilts by several makers that descended within one Sarahsville family.

Asymmetrical Sprig

Except for the central block, the field patterns in illustration 47 are Asymmetrical Sprigs. While they are related by the shapes of the flowers and leaves, the size of the units, and the red, green, and white color scheme, the lack of exact symmetry provides a delightful feeling of freedom in Grandma Sarah Jane Beatty's quilt, rather like an informal garden in full bloom.

As these examples indicate, the variety of classic floral quilts is almost limitless; yet the number of basic structures are few. Crosses, Floral Stars, Rosettes, and Prince's Feathers are radially symmetrical, with design elements aligned along various intersecting axes of the basic quilt block. The bilaterally symmetrical Floral Vase structure extends to such containers as baskets and vestigial flower holders. Each of these structures has antecedents in historical ornaments of many cultures throughout the world, from Romanian embroidered costumes and Czech Easter eggs to sophisticated Greek temples and Gothic cathedrals.

Design Influences

and Shared Style

48. Catherine Grill's Quilt, 1850–1875. Catherine Swigart Grill (1834–1920), Sharon Township (Medina County), Ohio. Cross or Floral Star structure, straight set, appliquéd. Cotton. 95" x 94". Collection of Bertha and Ervin Young.

Catherine Swigart and her husband, Daniel Grill, were both of Pennsylvania German background, which may account for the bold central motifs in her quilt blocks. Daniel farmed and operated a sawmill in Sharon. The Grills owned property adjoining the family farm of Ruth Finley, author of the 1929 classic, *Old Patchwork Quilts and the Women Who Made Them.* This farm, complete with c. 1840 farmhouse, is still in the family. Although Finley spent summers in Sharon and began collecting quilts there, she evidently missed this one made by her neighbor.

One of the most intriguing aspects of the classic floral quilt style is the consistency of subject matter. A quiltmaker can cut any shape she chooses for use on an appliquéd quilt, yet almost without exception the makers of these quilts selected botanical motifs as their primary theme.

Of course, flowers have been popular decorative motifs for centuries, and a glance at the current catalogs of any department store confirms that they continue to decorate bedding, china, and clothing. A variety of floral design influences was equally available to nineteenth-century quiltmakers, particularly gardens, other textiles, architecture, and decorative arts.

Flowers

As noted in "Classic Floral Quilts," flowers were especially popular with quiltmakers during the mid-nineteenth century. In her article on floral quilts in the Midsouth, Bets Ramsey notes the effect of terrain and horticulture on quiltmaking practices in that region. Especially during the Civil War, southern women looked to flowers for solace, "the one trait of civilization left after the hardening, barbarizing influence of the horrid war," as one Tennessee woman reported.[1]

Although the effect of the Civil War on northern women was different, they also lived in a rural environment and their letters and diaries attest to a love of flowers. American women everywhere created flower gardens. Such flowers as rose of Sharon, Harrison's rose, Michigan rose, Kentucky rose, prince's feather, and coxcomb were available through seed catalogs of the time.[2]

Mid-nineteenth-century women named some of their

49. Four generations of the quilt-maker's family
Catherine Swigart Grill (*right*) with her daughter, Amanda Grill Young, grandson Ervin Young, and great-grandson, Howard Young.

quilt patterns after these and other popular flowers. Irene Hardy, recalling her Ohio childhood in the 1840s and 1850s, wrote:

> . . . young women made quilts of bright-colored calicoes, bought for the purpose and cut into various intricate designs, which were sewed down, or applied on white cotton cloth. Months of work were often sewed into the closely wrought and elaborately quilted designs. Such quilts were much admired and usually put upon the best beds on great occasions. The designs often had fanciful names, as "Mary's Dream," "Morning Star," "Rose of Sharon."

Jane Shelby of Mississippi inked the name of her pattern, Mississippi Beauty, on the back of her 1855 classic floral quilt, and Sarah Robbins of Kentucky quilted the name of hers—Oregon Rose—on the quilt she made in 1851, the year she migrated to Oregon. It is important to remember, however, that unless we have evidence linking a particular quilt to the name used by its maker, we have no way of knowing what pattern name, if any, she used.[3]

In addition to seed catalogs, mid-nineteenth-century writers published numerous books and magazines on gardening, landscape design, and the symbolic language of flowers, through which one could communicate everything from acceptance of a suitor to the death of a child. European publications, such as J. C. Lou-

50. Architectural Garden Plans
Encyclopaedia of Cottage, Farm, and Villa Architecture
J. C. Loudon, 1842
Oberlin College Library

don's renowned *Encyclopaedia of Gardening,* were available in this country but needed modifications to be useful in America, with its varied climates and native plants.[4]

Andrew Jackson Downing, an admirer of Loudon's, was probably America's most influential exponent of home beautification; he published copiously on architecture and landscape gardening. He also urged his readers to grow plants indoors; some of his cottages included bay windows and conservatories for that purpose.

In *Cottage Residences,* along with architectural views and floor plans, Downing published designs for flower gardens, complete with recommended plantings. Borrowed from Loudon, these "architectural," "geometric," or "fancy gardens" were specifically designed to imitate ribbons and oriental carpets (see illustration 50). At the same time quilts reflected gardens, gardens imitated textiles. Geometric garden plans

51. Gardening
Amateur Cultivator's Guide, 1869
University of Delaware Library

were republished in America throughout the century in seed catalogs, gardening books, and magazines, as well as in Downing's writings.[5]

Of particular importance to quiltmakers, Downing repeatedly directed his advice to "the ladies of the household," believing flower gardening to be both "conducive to their own health, and to the beauty and interest of our homes." To further encourage the ladies, in 1843 Downing edited and published an American edition of *Gardening for Ladies, and Ladies' Companion to the Flower Garden,* a book written by Mrs. Loudon for amateur gardeners. Other writers throughout the century stressed the role of gardening in the development of taste, religion, purity, and good parenting. With such ties to the cult of domesticity, how could any woman resist?[6]

From the 1850s on, *Godey's Lady's Book* regularly reprinted sections of Loudon's books (including plans for geometric gardens), as well as botanical articles for women, such as "Botany As a Study for Young Ladies." Agricultural fair records from the same period report women winning premiums for cut flowers, artificial flowers, wax flowers, hair flowers, feather flowers, flower paintings, and "white quilts with sett [*sic*] flowers."[7]

A related influence on classic floral quilts was the enormous popularity of botany, or "botanizing," as its practitioners called it. From the mid-1830s until the mid-1880s, the study and collection of botanical specimens was America's most popular science. Involving professionals and amateurs alike, botany was both a scholastic discipline and an enjoyable recreation for enthusiasts of all ages.[8]

Botanizing was considered especially suitable for women and children. Through the collection and study of botanical specimens, children would develop skills of observation, engage in healthful exercise, learn orderly habits, and improve character. For ladies, botanizing was recommended as a genteel activity that inspired piety and led to such appropriately feminine occupations as flower painting and the creation of skeleton leaves and wax flowers. And women were ardent botanizers. As early as 1822 one writer observed that "more than half the botanists in New-England and New-York are ladies," and in 1887 an article in *Science* entitled "Is Botany a Suitable Study for Young Men?" assured readers that "able-bodied and vigorous brained young men" could indeed benefit from such an intellectual discipline.[9]

52. Jacquard Coverlet, 1837
Charles Meily, Wayne County, Ohio
The Ohio Historical Society

Textiles: Commercial

Other textiles also echoed the patterns of classic floral quilts. The most obvious of these is the Jacquard coverlet, popular from the 1830s until after the Civil War—at exactly the same time as these quilts (see illustrations 52 and 53). The two bedcovers have much in common.

Like classic floral quilts, Jacquard coverlets consist of a field of repeated blocks surrounded by a related border. The field patterns are botanical, conventionalized, and radially symmetrical, aligned along vertical, horizontal, and diagonal axes. The field often includes a secondary pattern, as is true of some quilts (see illustration 54).

53. Coxcomb and Blazing Star, 1850–1875. Maker unknown, Marshallville (Wayne County), Ohio. Cross structure, straight set, appliquéd, pieced, embroidered. Cotton. 94" x 92". Collection of Ila Stevic.

Four weavers worked in Marshallville, then called Bristol (Baughman Township), according to the 1850 census for Wayne County. At least one of them, Benjamin Lichty, wove Jacquard coverlets (see illustration 58). This dramatic quilt, whose field pattern is similar to the coverlet pattern in Illustration 52, was made for Winfield Scott Wertz by an unidentified neighbor. This quiltmaker created each of her field patterns from four smaller Symmetrical Bouquet blocks arranged in a square, with a sunburst placed in the center.

54. Rose Wreath, 1850–1875. Anna Stoneberger Rudy (1830–1923), Auglaize Township (Allen County), Ohio. Floral Wreath structure, diagonal set, appliquéd, piping inset. Cotton. 90" x 88". Collection of Betty and Dexter Beattley.

Anna Rudy and her husband, Shepherd Rudy, were both of Pennsylvania German background. They owned a 160-acre farm where they raised ten children. Anna Rudy's quilt has both primary and secondary field patterns, like many Jacquard coverlets. Rudy made quilts in several styles. An unusual feature of this one is the clear, bright yellow.

Borders are related by color and, as with the quilt borders, may include design units not used in the field patterns. Coverlet borders, in fact, are sometimes entirely unrelated to field patterns (see illustration 58). Most important, while both field and border patterns vary, as they do in the quilts, virtually every design structure in classic floral quilts is also found in Jacquard coverlets (see illustration 56).

56. Coverlet borders
The Ohio Historical Society

55. Anna Stoneberger Rudy

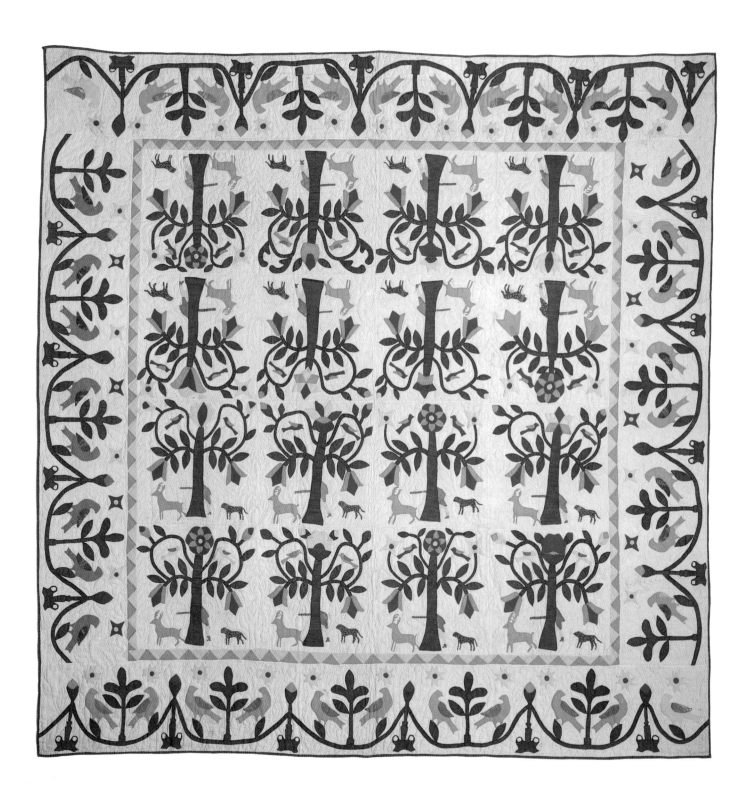

57. The Hunter Quilt, c. 1850. Maker unknown, Pennsylvania or Ohio. Symmetrical Bouquet structure with variations, straight set, appliquéd, pieced. Cotton. 83" x 83". The Ohio Historical Society.

This quilt exhibits a number of design influences from other textiles. The most obvious is the border, whose confronting birds and swags and tassels might have been taken directly from the borders of the Ardner coverlet in Illustration 56. The bilaterally symmetrical structure of the trees is similar to designs in samplers, as well as in the corner block of the coverlet in Illustration 58. The hunting scene in this quilt and the one in Illustration 11 were probably influenced by late-eighteenth-century copper-plate printed fabrics, whose subjects included historical, rural, patriotic, and hunting scenes.

Some patterns, such as the Coxcomb, Prince's Feather, Eight-pointed Star, Confronting Birds, and Sunburst are also common to both textiles. The central designs in many Floral Star quilts are nearly identical to one that was particularly popular in Jacquard coverlets (see illustration 58).[10]

Jacquard coverlets, known in the nineteenth century as "fancy coverlets," "flowered coverlets," and "carpet coverlets," were made primarily in Maryland, New York, Pennsylvania, Ohio, and Indiana. Most coverlet weavers in Pennsylvania and Ohio, where many classic floral quilts were made,

58. Jacquard Coverlet
Benjamin Lichty, Bristol (Marshallville, Wayne County), Ohio, 1840
Collection of Ila Stevic.

THE LIMA
Coverlet & Carpet Factory
STILL IN OPERATION.

The undersigned respectfully informs the public of Allen and the adjoining counties, that he still carried on the above business, and feels confident that he can render full satisfaction to all that may favor him with their patronage, provided always, that the materials are good, and prepared according to the following directions.

The quantity of yarn for one coverlet is twenty-four cuts of warp, no. 9 or 10, single cotton, of which 16 cuts must be three double, and eight cuts two double. The two double must be colored blue; this is sufficient where there are two or more in a web, where only one in a web, twenty-seven cuts is necessary.

• For filling, from 18 to 20 cuts of woollen yarn double and twisted, and one pound of single cotton, no. 9 or 10, the wool should be spun ten cuts to the pound, with a slight twist.

Coloring done to order.

Cotton, coverlet, and carpet warp, already doubled and twisted, can be purchased at the different stores in Lima.

His shop on Main street, north of the Public Square. JOHN H. MEILY.

March 23, 1847.

59. *The Lima Argus,* March 23, 1847 Allen County (Ohio) Historical Society

were Germanic migrants or German immigrants. Some coverlet weavers also produced ingrain carpet, using identical or similar patterns in both products. These elaborate design schemes were made possible by the development of a new aid to the professional weaver, the Jacquard attachment, which greatly increased the possibility of weaving complex patterns economically. With this new technological marvel, a professional could easily create realistic designs, lettering, and fancy ornaments.[11]

An improvement to the Jacquard mechanism in the 1840s permitted larger design repeats. This may account for the quadrant arrangement of field patterns in many classic floral quilts, a new departure in quilt design at this time. Carpets with large-scale floral patterns are also documented in paintings of the period.[12]

Jacquard coverlets bridged the gap between domestic and commercial textile production. They were produced by professional weavers, almost exclusively men. In some cases, however, they were woven to order from wool provided by the customer, who raised the sheep, spun the yarn, and perhaps dyed it. Spinning and home-dyeing were traditionally women's tasks. To help customers who supplied their own yarn, weavers sometimes included in their advertisements specific amounts and colors required (see illustration 59). This domestic aspect of coverlet production probably explains why women and an occasional "miss under sixteen" won premiums for the "best" and "second best double carpet coverlets" at agricultural fairs, along with professional weavers.[13]

At fairs Jacquard coverlets were displayed in a "domestic hall," along with quilts and other examples of needlework, where quiltmakers could readily see them. Although a woman who admired a Jacquard coverlet might not be able to weave one herself, she could make a quilt, basing her patterns on motifs and organization of design elements she saw in a coverlet that appealed to her.

Textiles: Domestic

Patterns on domestic textiles are also similar to quilt designs. Embroidered samplers almost always include floral units and meandering vine borders (see illustration 60). Many include pots of flowers, eight-pointed stars, and other bilaterally symmetrical units. These designs have a long history in the traditional arts of many cultures, where they decorated pottery, metalwork, paper, and furniture, as well as textiles.

When worked on fabric, their symmetry was often structurally determined. Early nee-

dle lace patterns, for instance, used the warp and weft threads of the base fabric, and Renaissance lace patterns required vertical, horizontal, or diagonal bars to join units and hold the lace flat (see illustration 61).[14]

This is also true of samplers embroidered in counted cross-stitch. Because the stitches cross the intersections of the vertical warp and horizontal weft, straight lines can be worked only in vertical, horizontal, or diagonal directions. The meandering vine borders of Eliza Rogers's sampler are angular for this reason (see illustration 60).

61. Renaissance lace patterns
The Unusual and New Designs . . . for all sorts of Needlework
Signor Federico [de] Vinciolo, 1606

60. Sampler, 1830. Eliza P. Rogers, Sutton Township (Meigs County), Ohio
The Ohio Historical Society

ELIZAHENRY✧ᶠH+D+H◁+Λ+F⊤ M+F ○ P F‡ M Λ❈H˚ G+ᶜ Ç ◎*M+E+C‡I8○

63. Inscription on Eliza Henry's quilt
The College of Wooster Art Museum

It is interesting to note that when quiltmakers like Eliza Henry transferred these designs to appliqué, where the structure of the base material is irrelevant, they still maintained the symmetry of these units.

Architecture

Architecture was another rich design source available to quiltmakers. Pioneers moving westward along the advancing frontier could neither rent nor purchase vacant homes as we do today; such homes simply didn't exist. Instead, the pioneers built temporary shelters until they could replicate their homes in the East or build in new styles.

Few migrants were architects, but local carpenters had

62. Rose Appliqué, c. 1840. Eliza Henry (Kline) (1822–1865), Wooster or Wayne Township (Wayne County), Ohio. Rosette structure, straight set, appliquéd, reverse appliquéd, embroidered. Cotton. Signed in embroidery. 89" x 81". Collection of Sylvia Eshelman.

Eliza Henry may have made this quilt in 1840 when she was eighteen. A still undeciphered inscription embroidered in the sashwork at the bottom of the quilt ends with the number 18, which may refer to her age. Her border design is closely related to several motifs on her sampler.

64. Motif from Eliza Henry's cross-stitch sampler

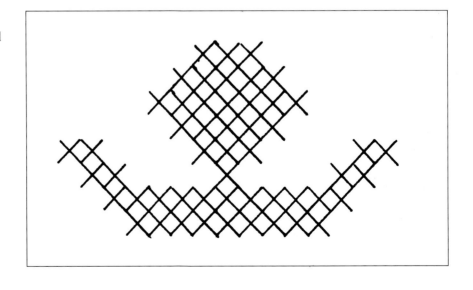

65. Currants and Coxcombs, 1842. Lucy Richards (Adams) (b. 1818), Suffield Township (Portage County), Ohio. Floral Star structure, diagonal set, appliquéd, embroidered. Cotton. 90" x 95". Courtesy of the Summit County Historical Society.

Lucy Richards was born in New Hampshire in 1818. By 1842, the year she made this quilt and married farmer Horace Adams, she was living in Portage County in Ohio's Western Reserve, a region settled by New Englanders. Lucy and Horace had five children. Lucy's quilt includes two designs also common to Greek Revival architecture, a style that was popular in the North at this time. Those motifs are the anthemion ornament (called coxcomb by quiltmakers) and the S-shaped vine or curve flanking a central motif. In architecture the central motif was usually an anthemion or acanthus leaf; in quilts it was almost always a flower-filled urn or basket.

access to a burgeoning number of building guides written by architects and published in America during this period: twenty between 1800 and 1840, sixty in the next twenty years, and fifty-eight in the 1870s. These guides promoted various architectural styles. The Greek Revival style, published in guides by architects Asher Benjamin and Minard Lafever, peaked in the 1830s and 1840s, and classical motifs were found in many middle- and upper-class Yankee homes. Makers of classic floral quilts apparently preferred this style, for they incorporated into their quilts such classical devices as rosettes, floral stars, swags and tassels, anthemion ornaments, and S-shaped curves flanking a central motif (see illustration 65).[15]

Quiltmakers didn't have to enter these lovely homes to appreciate the architectural details. They saw them every time they passed the structures, for builders lavished their greatest attention on doorways, which were profusely decorated in a variety of carved ornaments (see illustration 66).

66. Greek Revival doorway, Sharon Township (Medina County), Ohio
The swags and tassels, inverted anthemia, and dentils are Greek Revival motifs. The costumed lady at her spinning wheel that decorates the recently added screen door is pure Colonial Revival.

Decorative Arts and Interior Decoration

Similar patterns surrounded ladies within their homes; a common design vocabulary permeated all aspects of their lives. Floral wreaths edged dinner plates; rosettes and floral vases decorated furniture, mantles, and ceilings; swags bordered carpets and wallpaper and framed windows.

Publications

Interior decorating advice was transmitted through publications, which proliferated after 1840. Just as builders' guides were written in response to the need for architectural drawings in the expanding West, so an increasing number of household guides and advice books were written for women. These may have been particularly useful to those who had joined the westward migration, leaving behind the mothers and aunts who had earlier imparted their advice and training directly.[16]

67. Plaster ceiling ornaments
Encyclopaedia of Cottage, Farm, and Villa Architecture
A. J. Loudon, 1842
Oberlin College Library

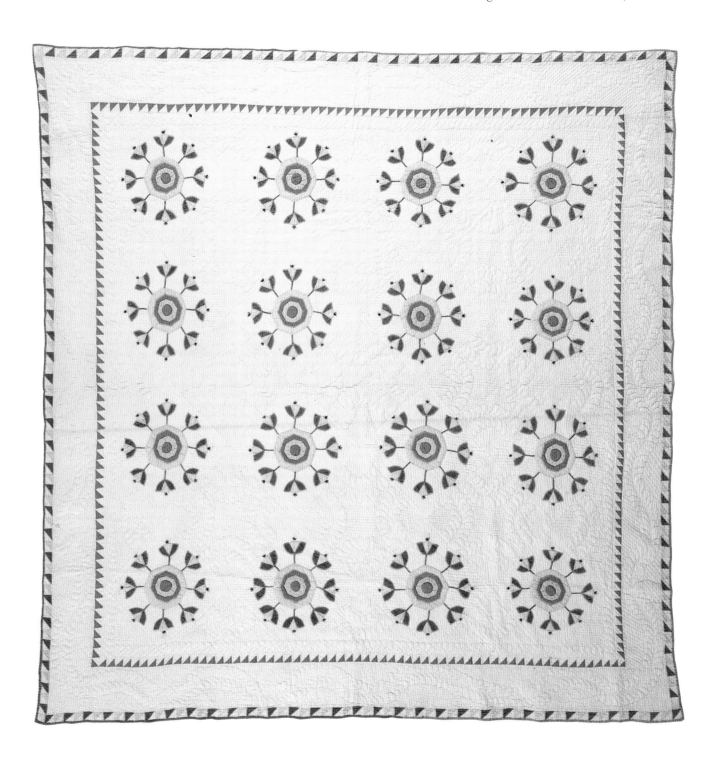

68. Rose, 1860–1865. Jennie Brown Brunton, Camba (Jackson County), Ohio. Rosette structure, straight set, appliquéd, pieced, reverse appliquéd, embroidered, embellished with machine chain stitch. Cotton. *76" x 74".* Collection of Charlotte Davis Specht.

Photo courtesy the Ohio Quilt Research Project.

Jennie Brunton made this quilt while her husband was serving in the Civil War.

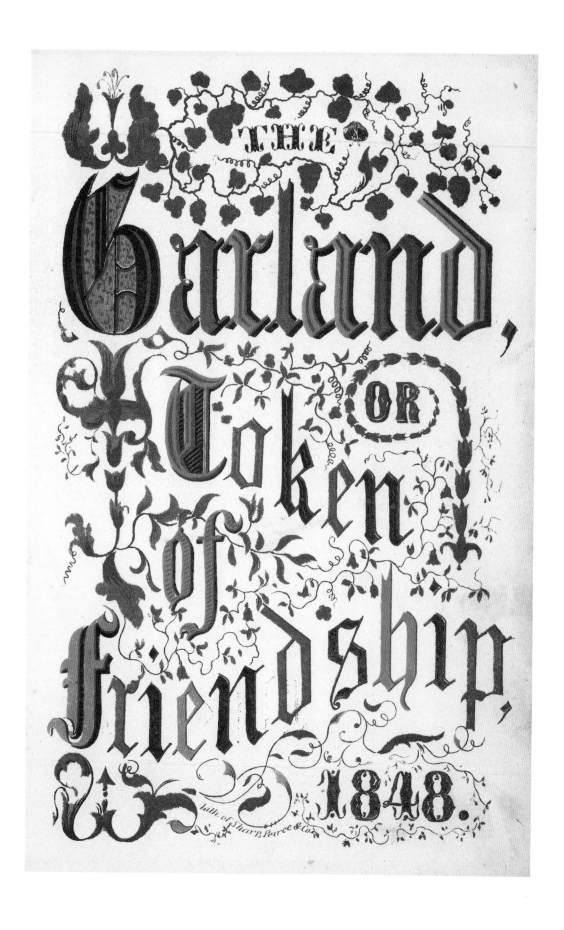

Published interior decorating advice may also account for the consistent color scheme. Although various "authorities" had different recommendations (the editor of *Godey's* admitted to being "puzzled as to which is the best rule to follow"), most relied on an earlier book by Scotsman David Ramsay Hay, *The Laws of Harmonious Colouring* (1828), when recommending appropriate colors. Hay advised using either of two color schemes, "harmony by analogy" or "harmony by contrast." The latter, based on complementary colors, was extremely popular in America and was the overwhelming choice of makers of classic floral quilts.[17]

The Ohio Quilt Research Project documented two classic floral quilts worked in blue and gold; all others were predominantly red and green (see illustration 68). Both schemes create "harmony by contrast."

The popularity of the red and green decorating scheme is documented in numerous paintings of the period, mostly of upper-class interiors. Many of these paintings were displayed in public exhibitions. Women also had access to inexpensive chromolithographs like those regularly included in the popular ladies' annual *The Garland* (see illustration 69).[18]

Popular magazines like *Godey's* regularly reprinted needlework designs from

69. *The Garland, or Token of Friendship 1848*
Chromolithograph, Warshaw Collection, Archives Center, National Museum of American History, the Smithsonian Institution

BRAID PATTERNS FOR APRONS.

ORNAMENTED aprons being once more in vogue, we selected a braid pattern that is both new and graceful. It should be done with the new style of

curled braid, and will have a richer effect than the common flat twist. The border encircles the apron, which should be only one rather wide breadth.

70. *Godey's Lady's Book,* January 1853
Oberlin College Library, Special Collections

71. Vorschrift (writing specimen), 1842
From the Hostetter Collection, the Leonard and Mildred Rothman Gallery, Franklin and Marshall College, Lancaster, Pennsylvania

English books and periodicals, as well as floral designs similar to the field patterns in classic floral quilts, such as ceiling medallions, garden plans, and designs on cottage furniture. The impact of interior decorating advice on a particular population is difficult to assess. By the early 1860s, however, 150,000 Americans subscribed to *Godey's Lady's Book* and were thus exposed to the decorating advice of Loudon and Hay, as well as to the floral designs of its needlework editor.[19]

One group of quiltmaking women may have had additional reasons for preferring classic floral quilts. Researchers in both Ohio and Kansas report a large number of Germanic quiltmakers working in this style. Those in Ohio were disproportionate to the state's quiltmaking population. Some of the design influences discussed above may explain why so many Germanic women made classic floral quilts.[20]

First, as noted by Clark and Hornback, bright colors and similar motifs were already a part of the Germanic decorative arts tradition (see illustration 71). Germanic quiltmakers were surrounded in their homes by painted furniture, incised earthenware, and colorful *frakturschriften* (decorated manuscripts). Women as well as men practiced the art of *fraktur* and also had a strong gender-based tradition of decorative textiles, including samplers and decorated hand towels. As noted above, Germanic quiltmaker Eliza Henry Kline's border designs are taken directly from her sampler. Some needlework tools, such as tape looms, were also decorated with brightly painted flowers.[21]

Further, as discussed earlier, most of the Jacquard coverlet weavers in Pennsylvania and Ohio, where so many of these quilts were made, were Germanic. Even the small town of Marshallville/Bristol in Baughman Township, Wayne County, had four weavers in 1850: two born in Pennsylvania and two born in Germany.[22] The communities in which these weavers settled provided a ready market for their coverlets, many of which included familiar Germanic designs, such as bird-and-bush borders and pots of flowers.[23]

Design sources for classic floral quilts were everywhere; they constituted the vocabulary of a shared cultural style. Flowers grew in gardens and decorated doorways, ceilings, carpets, coverlets, furniture, and china. Women collected them and replicated them in embroidery, wax, feathers, and hair. Flowers were the chief topic of countless books and magazines that also advised women on appropriate color schemes for their homes. Classic floral quilts are evidence that, at least in their bedrooms, women preferred complementary colors.

For Germanic women especially, brightly colored, symmetrical floral motifs were a continuing part of their domestic cultural tradition and influenced design wherever they located.

Spreading the Word

Dissemination of Style and Patterns

72. Rose of Sharon, 1855. Emily Fidler (b. 1832), Middlebury Township (Knox County), Ohio. Floral Star structure, straight set, appliquéd. Cotton. Signed and dated in quilting. 87" x 85". From a private collection.

Emily Fidler was one of twelve children in the Fidler family. Her father was a farmer who came from Pennsylvania; her mother was born in New Jersey. Emily had died by 1881, and her quilt was preserved by her sister, Deliah, and handed down in the family. Emily had quilted *Emily Fidler AD 1855* into a corner. Emily's quilt pattern is one of the most widely disseminated in the classic floral style. Examples still exist made in southern, northern, and midwestern states.

If asked to guess where Emily Fidler's quilt (illustration 72) was made, even a knowledgeable quilt researcher might have a difficult time deciding. Actually, Fidler made her quilt in Knox County, Ohio, in 1855, but quilts with nearly identical field patterns were made during the same period, not only throughout Ohio but in states as far apart as Alabama, Vermont, Pennsylvania, and Illinois (see illustration 15).

Although some quilt patterns were published in *Godey's Lady's Book* in 1855, few were for appliqué, and Fidler's was not among them. How did this pattern spread so far, well before the publication of patterns in agricultural journals and newspapers?[1]

One way, documented by Bets Ramsey, is through patterns that were handed down in families or exchanged by post. However, the existence more than a century later of so many similar quilts made over such a wide area suggests other means of dissemination of quilt styles and patterns.[2]

Even more intriguing than the well-known pattern in Emily Fidler's quilt are unusual, but similar, quilts. A pair of quilts by Mary Ann Burson Ward and Emma Ann Covert is a case in point.

Mary Ann Ward lived in Hendrysburg, Belmont County, in southeastern Ohio, and probably made her quilt between 1845 and 1850. Covert's quilt, made in Lebanon, Warren County (southwestern Ohio), is dated circa 1842 by Carrie Hall and Rose Kretsinger, who published it in 1935 in *The Romance of the Patchwork Quilt in America* (see illustrations 73 and 74). The quiltmakers were not related, and there is no reason to believe they knew each other.

73. Bowl of Flowers, c. 1850. Mary Ann Burson Ward (1832–1886), Hendrysburg (Belmont County), Ohio. Sampler, straight set, appliquéd, embroidered. Cotton. 87" x 85". Collection of Kaye Schneider, great-great-granddaughter of maker.

Mary Ann Burson was one of eight children of Amos and Eliza Burson. Both her father and her husband, George William Ward, were farmers. Her sampler quilt is unusual and invites comparison with Emma Covert's quilt in illustration 74. The fabrics that are now blue were probably originally green.

PLATE XXVI   *Courtesy Amy Ellen Hall*

BOUQUET OF GARDEN FLOWERS
This beautiful specimen of quilt-craft was made entirely by hand by Emma Ann Covert of Lebanon, Ohio, about 1842. A small figured print of green is used for the leaves, stems, small baskets, and bases of the large baskets, with red print for the flowers, buds, and large baskets. The design is appliqued on a fine homespun with a reversed buttonhole stitch and the quilting is done in the grape pattern. The owner of this valued heirloom is a granddaughter of the maker.

74. Bouquet of Garden Flowers, c. 1842. Emma Ann Covert, Lebanon (Warren County), Ohio. Sampler, straight set, appliquéd, embroidered. Cotton. Dimensions unknown. From Carrie A. Hall and Rose G. Kretsinger, *The Romance of the Patchwork Quilt in America* (Bonanza Books, 1935). With the permission of Dover Publications, Inc.

Both this quilt and Mary Ward's (Illustration 73) have red and green/blue in the same motifs. These are the only colors in Covert's quilt, whereas some of Ward's flowers are yellow. There is sashwork in both quilts. The grape pattern in Covert's quilting may refer to an undulating vine in the sashwork. In Ward's quilt, this area is quilted in a straight vine pattern.

75. Coxcomb, 1850–1875. Family of Theressa Marshall (1865–1941), Hocking or Carroll County, Ohio. Floral Star structure, straight set, appliquéd, reverse appliquéd, embroidered. Cotton. Initialed in embroidery. 93" x 85". From the collection of the Stark County Historical Society, Canton, Ohio.

Theressa Marshall (known as "Ressa" or "Aunt Ressie") was noted as a fine quiltmaker and a "saver who used up every last bit of thread when she sewed." She never married and with her brother operated a hotel in Dellroy, Ohio. Although this quilt is attributed to Ressa Marshall, whose initials are embroidered on the back, it may be a generation older. The green fabric is colored by an early, two-stage dye process, and the yellow printed material is identical to that used in another quilt made in the 1850s in Ohio.

Even though careful comparison of those quilts reveals that they are not identical, the overall plan and identical arrangement of field patterns suggest either a common source or the likelihood that one woman had seen the other's quilt. A third example, begun in 1852 by Hannah Johnson [Haines] of Indiana, was reportedly based on one she had seen in Ohio. This quilt appears as Plate 80 in *History From the Heart: Quilt Paths Across Illinois,* by E. Duane Elbert and Rachel Kamm Elbert.

Another pair of quilts further suggests that one woman tried to replicate a quilt she saw, but without access to the templates (see illustrations 75 and 77). The quilt in illustration 75 is from the family of Theressa ("Ressa") Marshall of

76. Margaret Black Marshall and her daughter, Theressa ("Ressa") Marshall

Carroll County, Ohio. The other, whose history is unknown, is estimated to have been made circa 1850.

Except for the borders, which reveal each quiltmaker's personal preference, everything about these quilts suggests that one was the model for the other, or that both had a common source. The branches along the diagonal axes sprout one large flower and a secondary branch with a smaller one, one large and two small leaves, and two branches with berries near the base. In each quilt one long, curving leaf lies along the vertical and horizontal axes. The central motif in each is designed by cutting a folded pattern from paper or cloth, extended at the corners and indented at the sides. Each of these designs has a smaller paper-cut motif at its center.

Each quiltmaker created details through reverse appliqué; in some cases, the number and placement of slits in corresponding pieces are identical in both quilts. Finally, not only are the same colors used throughout, but in each quilt the red and green fabrics are solid, and the yellow is a print.

The similarities and differences in each of these pairs of quilts are exactly what we might expect when an observant quiltmaker decided to replicate a quilt she saw only at a distance and whose patterns she could only sketch.

77. Coxcomb, c. 1850. Maker unknown, place unknown. Floral Star structure, straight set, appliquéd, reverse appliquéd, embroidered. Cotton. 86" x 86". *The Quilt Engagement Calendar.*

Except for the clearly different borders, these unusual quilts are quite similar. Both quiltmakers carried the coxcomb motifs into their borders but used them in entirely different ways.

The widely dispersed Rose of Sharon pattern and these pairs of unusual, yet related, quilts raise additional questions about the transmission of quilt styles and patterns. Quiltmakers were apparently exposed to classic floral quilts well beyond those made by relatives or neighbors. As these quilts were neither described nor illustrated in the popular press before the 1880s, there must have been another means of proliferation. There are two major ways I believe such patterns were disseminated: regionally, through agricultural fairs; and nationally, along migration routes.

The Agricultural Fair

The chief social, educational, and recreational event in rural America in the mid-nineteenth century was the agricultural fair, whose chief purpose was the advancement of agriculture through education, with standards set through competition. Rather than relying on descriptions in agricultural journals, farmers attending fairs could actually inspect the newest breeds of sheep, the hardiest varieties of wheat, and the latest improved cultivator, while their wives and daughters saw "mounds of dahlias," "woolen hose carded, spun and knitted by the exhibitor," and the newest sewing machines.[3]

Fairs were sponsored by agricultural societies, a British institution reinstated by descen-

78. Broadside, Ohio, 1852
The Western Reserve Historical Society, Cleveland, Ohio.

The "Equestrian Performance by Ladies" was a popular and highly controversial activity at agricultural fairs. Many fair boards felt forced to establish a policy on whether or not to include "equestriennes" and defended their position in their annual reports.

dants of America's English settlers. The most successful of these societies were based on a model developed in 1810 by Elkanah Watson of Berkshire County, Massachusetts, who involved women as well as men and made the annual fair the societies' central activity. After the New York State legislature began funding its state and county societies in 1841, other states followed suit and American agricultural societies blossomed, particularly in the North.[4]

The agricultural society movement spread westward and was particularly strong in the Midwest. In 1858 the states then constituting that region (Illinois, Indiana, Iowa, Michigan, Minnesota, Missouri, Ohio, and Wisconsin), with 28 percent of the nation's population, boasted more than 48 percent of the agricultural societies in the United States. Prior to statehood, Minnesota, Nebraska, and South Dakota also held local or territorial fairs. By 1870, the midwestern states had 32 percent of the population and 55 percent of the agricultural societies. In contrast, the South, with roughly one-third of the nation's population, had only 18 percent of the agricultural societies in 1858 and 6 percent in 1868, no doubt because of the devastation of the Civil War.[5]

Golden Age of the Agricultural Fair

By midcentury, midwestern agricultural fairs were in full swing. Although the statistics are probably exaggerated, reporters throughout Ohio commented on the unprecedented numbers of spectators: 10,000 at the 1852 Columbiana County Fair, 12,000 to 15,000 at the 1855 Washington County Fair, 50,000 to 100,000 at the 1854 Ohio State Fair. On a single day in 1856, an estimated 15,000 attended a town fair in Claridon (Geauga County), population 1,000. The period from 1850 to 1870 was declared "the golden age of the agricultural fair."[6]

It is not by chance that this coincides with the golden age of the classic floral quilt. Several of the factors responsible were the same: mechanization, improved transportation, and the closing of the frontier. Just as machine spinning and power looms revolutionized the textile industry, so did the steel plow, reaper, threshing machine, corn planter, and cultivator—all developed between 1837 and 1850—revolutionize agriculture. And just as canals and railroads provided quiltmakers with more fabric at lower cost, so they also enabled farmers to transport livestock and farm machinery quickly and economically.

Until permanent fairgrounds could be constructed, fairs were held in different locations each year, thus enhancing publicity and doubtless increasing local enthusiasm. Although state fairs are better known

79. Champion Reaping and Mowing Machine: The Excelsior Reaper at Work in the Field
Twenty-second Annual Report of the Ohio State Board of Agriculture for 1867
Oberlin College Library

❧ Domestic Hall was really a bazaar of beauty. Almost every conceivable article of needle work was represented, in quality and numbers far superior to that of any previous fair.

Report of the Cuyahoga County (Ohio)
Agricultural Society
1869

today than local fairs, these larger events came later, building on an existing tradition of local fairs sponsored by county, town, or union agricultural societies that served isolated areas, typically "situated at the corner of four counties . . . twenty miles from the location of any county society."[7]

In 1860, in addition to the Ohio state and county fairs, Ashtabula County reported four independent fairs and Lorain County seven; in that year no Lorain County resident lived more than ten miles from the site of an agricultural fair. Later in the century, contiguous areas joined forces to add larger regional events such as the Northern, Southern, and Southwestern Ohio fairs; the Eastern Ohio and Western Pennsylvania Fair; and the Tri-State Fair, at the junction of Ohio, Michigan, and Indiana.[8]

Timing of fairs in any one region was usually staggered so everyone could attend several. Local fairs attracted visitors from surrounding communities. State fairs drew from even greater distances, in part because railroad companies "generously carried passengers upon extra trains at half price, and articles and stock intended for exhibition, free of charge." The list of premium winners at the first Ohio State Fair, held in Cincinnati in 1850, includes residents of thirty-six Ohio counties, ten other states as far away as Alabama and Vermont, and Canada.[9]

Domestic Hall: A Bazaar of Beauty

As early as 1813, when Elkanah Watson offered fifteen premiums for domestic manufactures, women were strongly encouraged to participate in agricultural fairs. And so they did. Ohio women submitted more than half of the 1,502 entries at the 1865 Clermont County Fair. At the 1858 Cattle Show and Fair in Brunswick (Medina County), 135 of the 810 entries were in the Domestic Manufactures category, a number surpassed only by the catch-all Miscellaneous. Women's participation in agricultural fairs was considered so important that in 1852 the Washington County Agricultural Society applied the entire admission fees collected — $52.25 — to premiums in the Domestic Manufactures category.[10]

Reporters praised women for creating "Bazaars of Beauty," for the cult of domesticity decreed that women were responsible for "the cultivation of taste." This was not taken lightly; a journalist writing for the *Ohio Farmer* after the 1856 state fair identified *taste* as one of four significant results of the state fair, adding that women's exhibitions "possess better qualities for stimulus and instruction, than the Louvre or Valhalla."[11]

80. Tulip Quilt, 1859–1860. Caroline Winters Bacon, Newark (Licking County), Ohio. Floral Star and Cross structures, straight set, appliquéd, piping inset. Cotton. 82" x 80". Licking County (Ohio) Historical Society.

Caroline Bacon was the wife of a physician and druggist in Newark. In 1859 or 1860 she entered this quilt in the Licking County Fair and took first prize of $10. These same years, first prize for a quilt at the Ohio State Fair was only $3. Newark, however, was a prosperous canal town and was better able to reward its quiltmakers.

Their entries—bread, butter, and preserves; handmade textiles, including quilts; flower arrangements and fancy articles—were exhibited together in Domestic Hall or Floral Hall, repeatedly described by reporters as "a splendid affair" and "the center of attraction."[12]

Quilts at agricultural fairs were fully visible, "extensively spread out" or "hung along on either side of the passage way." Extant prize-winning quilts and eyewitness descriptions indicate that classic floral quilts were prominent among those on view. Indeed, in the early 1860s the Union Agricultural Society of Lorain County established an entire category for classic floral quilts: "White quilts with sett [*sic*] flowers." A "Figured bed quilt" category at the second Ross County Agricultural Society Fair in 1847 may also refer to this style.[13]

Visitors to the Ohio State fairs in 1864 and 1865 would have seen Nancy Meeker's quilt, judged the Best Patchwork Quilt each of those years. This quilt and others would have been prominently displayed before the "scores of thousands of visitors" who attended the state fairs in those years. Quiltmakers who wanted to make a quilt like Meeker's, similar in design to Emily Fidler's (see illustration 72), could study it over the three days of the fair, sketch the pattern, and approximate it.[14]

Because of the large number of fairs, their staggered dates, and their proximity, some women entered several fairs each year, thus increasing public exposure to their fine needlework. They exhibited numerous articles and won multiple premiums. At the Ashtabula County Fair of 1856, twenty-six of the thirty-eight premiums in the Family Manufactures and Linen Manufactures categories went to four women.

In 1865 Mercia Church of Painesville (Lake County) won fourteen premiums at the Lake County Fair and seventeen, totaling forty-one dollars, at the Ohio State Fair. Her impressive record at both fairs continued; and when the Northern Ohio Fair was established in 1870, she began exhibiting and winning premiums at those fairs as well.[15]

Church was talented but not unique. She had a strong competitor in Mary Sprague of Reynoldsburg (Franklin County), a model of domesticity even before she exhibited "in a large space . . . a multitude of specimens of her own handiwork, comprising embroidery, fine needle-work, etc." at the 1874 Fairfield County Fair. From 1864 on, Sprague won repeated awards at the Ohio State fairs, including twenty-three premiums worth eighty-nine dollars in 1868. Both women were award-winning quiltmakers. It

81. Rose of Sharon, 1840–1841. Nancy Simpson (Meeker) (b. 1822) and her mother, Mrs. Simpson, Richmondale (Ross County), Ohio. Cross structure, straight set, appliquéd, stuffed. Cotton. 83" x 84". The Ohio Historical Society.

Nancy Simpson Meeker and her mother made this quilt in anticipation of her 1842 wedding to Lemmon Meeker. The Meekers lived on their farm in Richmondale until the early 1860s, when they moved with their nine sons to Shadeville, south of

Columbus. In 1864 and 1865 the Ohio State fairs were held in Columbus, and Nancy exhibited this quilt both years. Each year it was awarded a $3 premium as the Best Patchwork Quilt (the term *appliqué* was not applied to quilts).

CUT FLOWERS.	
Best and largest collection 24 named Dahlias, John Kelley, Cleveland	5
2d best " " " Mrs. M. Church, Painesville	3
Best and largest collection 12 named Dahlias, same "	3
2d best " " " John Kelley, Cleveland	2
Best and largest collection of named Roses, Mrs. M. Church, Painesville	5
" " " Verbenas, same "	3
Best 12 Verbenas, Mrs. M. Church, Painesville	2
Best and largest collection of named Phloxes, Mrs. W. R. Sprague, Reynoldsburg	2
2d best " " " Mrs. M. Church, Painesville	1
Best display of Asters, Mrs. W. R. Sprague, Reynoldsburg	2
" " Gladiolus, Mrs. M. Church, Painesville	3
" " Coxcombs and Amaranths, Mrs. W. R. Sprague, Reynoldsburg	2
2d best " " " Mrs. M. Church, Painesville	1
Best and greatest display of cut flowers,other than above, Mrs.M. Church, Painesville.	5
2d best do., Mrs. W. R. Sprague, Reynoldsburg	3

82. Premium list, the *Twentieth Annual Report of the Ohio State Board of Agriculture for 1865*
Oberlin College Library

❧ LADIES' DEPARTMENT.— The ladies of our county are entitled to our lasting gratitude, for the commendable interest they took in the whole business of our fair, and their own department of it, was the observed of all observers. Such quilts, such embroideries, such needlework of all kinds; and then, such pyramids of flowers, such vases, such wreaths, such boquets [*sic*], such a vast variety in pots, the like has seldom been seen this side of Eden.

Warren County (Ohio) *Agricultural Report*
1852

is unlikely that they ever met, except perhaps at state fairs, but a glance at the premium list makes one wonder how they felt about each other (see illustration 82).[16]

Although fairs were intended to appeal to the competitive instinct in exhibitors, for women "'emulation, not envy,' was the sentiment which actuated their hearts." Their breads, preserves, flower arrangements, wax bouquets, and quilts were evaluated, first by a committee of their peers, then by the public. Winning a premium validated domesticity and rewarded those who best fulfilled their roles in recreating Paradise in their homes. The names of each community's most outstanding homemakers were known to thousands who read the lists of winners, and

the monetary rewards these women won were impressive.[17]

Fairs were a significant means of spreading quilt styles and patterns regionally. However, quilts made in the East were also entered later in fairs held in western states, as Virginia Gunn has noted, thus spreading regional patterns more widely.[18] The phenomenon of massive westward expansion in the nineteenth century is probably the major factor in the dissemination of all quilt styles and patterns.

Westward Migration

The earliest migration patterns were north and south, from the Middle Atlantic States along the eastern seaboard. We have already noted similarities among album quilts in sections

❧Never, since the organization of our Society, was the exhibition in this department so full and attractive; and, as an illustration of the industry of our Licking County ladies, it is simply necessary for me to say that one lady entered two hundred different articles for premiums, and several others from one hundred to one hundred and fifty articles. One lady was awarded the sum of $98 in premiums, being certainly a generous reward for merited perseverance.

Annual Report
Licking County (Ohio)
  Agricultural Society
1871

of Maryland, Pennsylvania, New Jersey, and New York, as well as a preference for yellow backgrounds both in southeastern Pennsylvania and in areas of North Carolina settled by Pennsylvanians.

Most nineteenth-century migration, however, was westward. Yankees moved from New England through New York and Pennsylvania, first into the Northwest Territory (Ohio, Indiana, Illinois, Michigan, Wisconsin, and part of Minnesota), then into the Midwest (Kansas, Nebraska, Oklahoma), and on to the Far West (California and Oregon). Southerners migrated from Virginia and the Carolinas through Tennessee, Kentucky, and Missouri into Texas or Kansas.

However, some migrants from the South moved north,

83. Emigration in 1817
S. G. Goodrich, *Recollections of a Lifetime*, 1856
Oberlin College Library

One of Mary's quilts she called "The Star and Crescent." I had never seen it before. She got the pattern from a Mrs. Lefferts, one of the new Pennsylvania Dutch families, and pieced it this winter. A lot of Dutch are taking up land here in the Reserve.

1841, from Ruth E. Finley
Old Patchwork Quilts and the Women Who Made Them
1929

and some from the North moved south. Cultural geographer Hubert Wilhelm has described Ohio in 1850 as "like the lower end of a funnel that widened into the interior and through which America's migrating masses were channeled." These "migrating masses" included quiltmaking women.[19]

When Cordelia Friedline moved with her husband, Charles, from Ohio to Kansas, her Princess Feather quilt was among the treasures she took with her (see illustration 84). After Charles discovered that farming on the "Great American Desert" was impossible, the Friedlines moved to Colorado. They lived first in Colorado Springs, then in Denver, where Charles established a grocery business. Eventually Cordelia's quilt returned to Ohio with her granddaughter.[20]

Sophia Totman's quilt also traveled (see illustration 86). Sophia made it in Ontario County, New York, and brought it with her when she and her husband, B. T. Luther, moved first to Michigan, and later to California.

When women like Cordelia Friedline and Sophia Totman Luther met migrating women from other eastern states, they saw quilt styles or patterns that may have been new to them. Because of the recent publications of so many

state quilt documentation projects, it is possible to find in most of these books quilts made in the East and carried west by migrating women. Many were in the classic floral style. Of 147 classic floral appliquéd quilts documented by the Kansas Quilt Project, the states of origin of 92 were identified. Only 6 were made in Kansas. The others came to Kansas from the East, primarily from Ohio (31), Indiana (14), and Illinois (10).[21]

These quilts would have been readily seen by interested quiltmakers, for frontier homes were small, with most of the families' possessions in full view. Further, visits were lengthy, and friends were involved in many more of their hostesses' activities than is true today. In her 1818 diary, Laura Clark of Wakeman, Ohio, refers frequently to long visits with her neighbors who lived only a short distance away. Because her physician husband was often gone for two or three days at a time, Laura Clark sometimes stayed overnight with neighbors: ". . . stayed with Lecta all day finished my bonnet . . . went to Canfields & stayed all night. . . . went to see Lecta & bake pumpkin pies—stayed all night." Eliza Farnham, writing about life on the Illinois frontier in the early 1840s, reported similar occasions, where visits began early in the afternoon and lasted until nearly 8:00 P.M.[22]

84. Princess Feather, 1850–1875. Attributed to Cordelia Moomaw Friedline (1843–1936), Frankfort (Ross County), Ohio. Prince's Feather structure, straight set, appliquéd, stuffed. Cotton. 92" x 94". From a private collection.

This deceptively simple quilt exhibits spectacular quilting technique. It is decorated with quilted, stuffed flowers and floral wreaths, baskets, and eagles, set off by areas of stipple quilting. According to family tradition, Cordelia made this quilt in Ohio and took it with her when she and her husband, Charles Friedline, went west to farm, first in Kansas, then in Colorado. Eventually Charles went into the grocery business in Denver. The Friedlines had two daughters.

Visitors scrupulously studied their neighbors' sewing projects and even borrowed them to "have the patterns taken." Irene Hardy, recalling her childhood in Eaton (Preble County), Ohio, during the 1840s reported:

Whenever a neighbor came to spend the day on a visit to my mother, a part of the entertainment consisted, as a matter of course, in showing her patchwork quilts, finished or in process of making, a piece of cloth in the loom, or lately woven, and any new garment made or in the making. In the same way, every quilt pieced and quilted in the neighborhood was known and spoken of in other houses.[23]

Although classic floral quilts were not made in frontier communities, they were among the treasures carried by westward-migrating women. Other women were interested in their neighbors' quilts and had ample opportunity to study them.

The classic floral quilt style spread well beyond families and neighborhoods. In settled areas, women entered them in agricultural fairs where they were judged by peers, then proudly displayed and viewed by multitudes. If a quiltmaker visiting a fair fell in love with a pieced quilt "hung on either

85. Cordelia Moomaw Friedline with grandsons Frank *(left)* **and Charles**

87. Sophia Totman and sisters with their husbands
Seated, *left to right:* Henry Reed, Catherine Totman Bliss, Benjamin T. Luther. Standing, *left to right:* Nancy Totman Reed, Philenzo Payne Bliss, and quiltmaker Sophia Totman Luther.

86. Flower Basket, before 1867. Sophia Irene Totman (1836–1927), Bristol (Ontario County), New York. Floral Vase structure, diagonal set, pieced, appliquéd. Cotton. Signed in appliqué. 82″ x 82″. Collection of Alice Clizbe.

After her 1867 marriage to Benjamin T. Luther, Sophia Totman took this quilt with her when they went west, living first in Michigan, then in California. The Luthers had two children, Alvah and Mary. That Sophia's quilt is in such pristine condition does not surprise Sophia's grand-niece Kay, who remembers that "Aunt Sophia was a real lady. She was always beautifully dressed, with a ribbon around the neck of a fresh, white blouse, even when she was at the farm."

side or across the passageway," she could easily reproduce a pieced design by analyzing the basic pattern into its component parts. Replicating an appliquéd quilt would be more challenging, but a determined quiltmaker could approximate an outstanding model.[24]

Because of the immense popularity of agricultural fairs before the publication of quilt patterns but during the period of the flowering of the classic floral quilt style, it is likely that fairs played a major role in the regional dispersal of that style.

Women also took classic floral quilts with them when they left their homes and migrated. They shared them with women they encountered along the way and in their new homes in the West, and they carefully preserved them. The fact that so many quilts in many styles have survived the rugged treks west is eloquent testimony to their significance to generations of women.

Conclusion

This study began with certain questions about the classic floral quilt style. Seeking—and occasionally finding—convincing answers has been enjoyable and rewarding. As so often happens in such a quest, it has also raised additional questions.

We know, for instance, that the makers of classic floral quilts were young women skilled at needlework and that their average age was twenty-three. Were youthful, talented seamstresses common in the mid-nineteenth century, or do we notice and admire these talents because they are rare today?

Unquestionably, women learned hand-sewing skills early. This quilt style was at its height of popularity before sewing machines were widely affordable. As they expected to make most of their families' clothing after marriage, quiltmakers would have begun

sewing, perhaps on Nine-Patch quilt tops, by the age of five. By their teen years, they would have been trained and experienced seamstresses. This may explain why quilt researchers in Kansas found so few appliquéd classic floral quilts actually made there: by the end of the frontier period in Kansas, most women were using sewing machines, and hand sewing had become a skill of the past.[1]

At the same time, it seems reasonable to assume that only those young women who genuinely enjoyed sewing made these decorative, labor-intensive quilts. This is particularly true of those quiltmakers who lavished their attention on stuffing and closely spaced stipple quilting, techniques that were entirely decorative and sometimes obviated the insulating function of quilts.

One rather curious aspect of classic floral quilts is the selective way the quiltmakers uti-

lized some patterns of the period but rejected others. The floral theme itself and the bright, contrasting colors have already been fully analyzed. Some field designs, especially rosettes and anthemion ornaments, as well as such border designs as swags and tassels and a floral motif flanked by S-curves, are shared with the Greek Revival architectural style.

One marvels, however, that the highly decorative pointed arches, trefoils, quatrefoils, and tracery designs characteristic of Gothic Revival architecture, coming into popularity at exactly the same time, played almost no role in these quilts.[2] This seems particularly remarkable when we remember that Gothic was considered "the architecture of Christianity" and that religion was the special province of women.

The persistent use of the tried and true may give us another insight into the psychological makeup of these women. They seem to have been traditional and conservative. Their reliance for more than forty years on centuries-old pattern structures and on an unusually rigid quilt style supports this. They were satisfied with familiar designs and patterns, a limited color scheme, and consistent subject matter. As I have tried to demonstrate, there is remarkable diversity within the classic floral style. Nevertheless, the personal choices these quiltmakers made in their selection of motifs, fabrics, and design structures were safe. They expressed originality within a specific, well-established context.

As is true of several examples included here, many of these quilts were made for special occasions and have been well preserved. Was commemoration a function of this style? As Irene Hardy noted in her memoirs of 1913, "Such quilts were much admired and usually put upon the best beds on great occasions." However, commemorative signature quilts in other styles, such as Yankee repeated-block pieced quilts and Baltimore album quilts, were popular at the same time, and probably as many were made during this same period to mark weddings, births, friendships, and departures. In this regard, the classic floral quilt style was probably not unusual.

However, classic floral quilts may have had one unique function. In writing of "plain painters," folklorist John Michael Vlach asserts that most nineteenth-century American folk paintings were "art produced for a newly emergent bourgeoisie anxious to acquire symbols of success." Classic floral quilts may have had a comparable role, as they were displayed competitively in agricultural fairs, incorporated elements of color, design, and interior decoration recommended by taste-setters, and were made in a settled, post-frontier environment. Classic floral quilts might be considered symbols of women's success as nurturers and angels, guardians of the home as Eden and as sanctuary.[3]

Notes

Classic Floral Quilts: The Makers and Their World

[1] Many classic floral quilts include secondary colors, such as yellow or pink.

[2] James N. Liles, "Dyes in American Quilts Made Prior to 1930, with Special Emphasis on Cotton and Linen," *Uncoverings 1984*, 37.

[3] Rabbit Goody, "Will the Real James Alexander Coverlets Please Stand Up," *The Clarion*, Spring 1992, 52–58.

[4] Benjamin Franklin, "The Internal State of America; Being a True Description of the Interest and Policy of That Vast Continent," *The Writings of Benjamin Franklin*, ed. Albert H. Smyth (New York: Macmillan Co. [1905–1907]), 10:117–118.

[5] J. Hector St. John Crevecoeur, *Letters from an American Farmer* (London, 1782; reprint, New York: Fox, Duffield & Company, 1904), 49–51; Henry Nash Smith, *Virgin Land: The American West as Symbol and Myth* (Cambridge: Harvard University Press, 1950); Thomas Jefferson, *Notes on the State of Virginia* (Philadelphia: H. C. Carey & I. Lea, 1825), 224; Leo Marx, *The Machine in the Garden: Technology and the Pastoral Ideal in America* (New York: Oxford University Press, 1964), ch. 3.

[6] Annette Kolodny, *The Land Before Her: Fantasy and Experience of the American Frontiers, 1630–1860* (Chapel Hill: University of North Carolina Press, 1984), 6; Morgan Reese, Philadelphia, 1796, in Howard Mumford Jones, *O Strange New World: American Culture: The Formative Years* (New York: Viking Press, [1964]), 212; Elisabeth Adams, Davenport, Iowa, to Ephraim Adams, Grinnell, Iowa, May 5, 1856. Quoted in Kolodny, *Land*, 177.

[7] Census records indicate that some of these quilt-makers had hired helpers as part of their households.

[8] Ricky Clark, George W. Knepper, and Ellice Ronsheim, *Quilts in Community: Ohio's Traditions* (Nashville: Rutledge Hill Press, 1991), 59–60.

[9] R. Carlyle Buley, *The Old Northwest: Pioneer Period 1815–1840* (Indianapolis: Indiana University Press, 1950), 1:534; George W. Knepper, *Ohio and Its People* (Kent, Ohio: Kent State University Press, 1989), 149–159; Rexford Newcomb, *Architecture of the Old Northwest Territory* (Chicago: University of Chicago Press, 1950), 42–43.

[10] Knepper, *Ohio*, 145–149, 160.

[11] Pat Ferrero, Elaine Hedges, and Julie Silber, *Hearts and Hands: The Influence of Women & Quilts on American Society* (San Francisco: The Quilt Digest Press, 1987), 22 ff.; "Editor's Table," *Godey's Lady's Book* 47 (July 1853), 84.

[12] Mrs. L. Maria Child, *The Girl's Own Book* (New York, 1833), quoted in "The Cult of True Woman-hood: 1820–1860," by Barbara Welter, *American Quarterly* 18 (1966), #165; Harvey Green, *The Light of the Home: An Intimate View of the Lives of Women in Victorian America* (New York: Pantheon Books, 1983), 36–37.

Themes and Variations: Related Styles

[1]Gloria Seaman Allen, *First Flowerings: Early Virginia Quilts* (Washington, DC: DAR Museum, 1987), 8, 18.

[2]Sally Garoutte, "Early Colonial Quilts in a Bedding Context," *Uncoverings 1980*, 18–27; Florence Montgomery, *Textiles in America, 1650–1870* (New York: W. W. Norton & Company, n.d.), 185–186.

[3]For a discussion of the development of the block-style quilt, see Jonathan Holstein, "The American Block Quilt," in Jeannette Lasansky, ed., *In the Heart of Pennsylvania: Symposium Papers* (Lewisburg, PA: The Oral Traditions Project, 1986), 16–26.

[4]Dena S. Katzenberg, *Baltimore Album Quilts* (Baltimore: The Baltimore Museum of Art, 1981), 60–65.

[5]Eleanor Sienkiewicz, "The Marketing of Mary Evans," *Uncoverings 1989*, 18.

[6]Lewis F. Day, *Nature in Ornament* (London: B. T. Batsford, 1892), 136; John Joseph Stoudt, *Pennsylvania Folk-Art* (Allentown, Pennsylvania: Schlechter's, 1948), 104 ff.; Alexander Speltz, *Style of Ornament Exhibited in Designs and Arranged in Historical Order with Descriptive Text* (Berlin: Bruno Hessling, [1906]), 43–66.

[7]Rita Erickson, letter to author, 7 August 1992.

[8]Phyllis Tepper, letter to author, 15 April 1993.

[9]Patricia Herr, letter to author, 9 October 1992; Polly Allison duPont, "Berks County Quilt Harvest—Is That a Quilt Show?", *Historical Review of Berks County*, 58:1 (Winter 1992–1993), 15; Jeannette Lasansky, letter to author, November 1992.

[10]Erma Kirkpatrick, letter to author, 5 November 1992. See also Ellen Fickling Eanes et al., *North Carolina Quilts* (Chapel Hill: University of North Carolina Press, 1988), 73, 92, plates 3–9, 3–12, 3–13, 3–25.

[11]These include the District of Columbia, Illinois, Indiana, Kentucky, Louisiana, Michigan, Missouri, Mississippi, South Carolina, and Tennessee. Both Donna Bister of Vermont and Linda Welter of Rhode Island found very few classic floral quilts made in their states, and Wendy Reed of the Maine Quilt Heritage found none at all.

[12]Ricky Clark et al., *Quilts in Community*, 14–16.

[13]*The Farm and Fireside*, 11 November 1882; *Godey's Lady's Book*, December 1887; Virginia Gunn, "Crazy Quilts and Outline Quilts: Popular Responses to the Decorative Art/Art Needlework Movement, 1876–1893," *Uncoverings 1984*, 131–152.

Roses or Carnations: The Quilt Patterns Analyzed

[1]The Princess Feather quilt pattern was one of the earliest appliqué patterns published, appearing in the September 15, 1883, *Farm and Fireside* (Springfield, Ohio), in response to a request from a reader. The respondent, Mrs. E. J. H. Moody of Kansas, recommended nine blocks. Her diagram and instructions were reprinted verbatim in "Aunt Jane's Prize Winning Quilt Designs" in 1914. This pamphlet was produced by *The Household Journal*, a successor to *Farm and Fireside*. See E. Duane Elbert and Rachel Kamm Elbert, *History from the Heart: Quilt Paths Across Illinois* (Nashville: Rutledge Hill Press, 1993), 145.

Design Influences and Shared Style

[1]Bets Ramsey, "Roses Real and Imaginary: Nineteenth-Century Botanical Quilts of the Mid-South," *Uncoverings 1986*, 9–25.

[2]Ann Leighton, *American Gardens of the Nineteenth Century: "For Comfort and Affluence"* (Amherst: University of Massachusetts Press, 1987), 299–378.

[3]Louis Filler, ed., *An Ohio Schoolmistress: The Memoirs of Irene Hardy* (Kent, Ohio: Kent State University Press, 1980), 71; Karoline Bresenhan and Nancy Puentes, *Lone Stars: A Legacy of Texas Quilts, 1836–1936* (Austin: University of Texas Press, 1986), 40; Mary Bywater Cross, *Treasures in the Trunk: Quilts of the Oregon Trail* (Nashville: Rutledge Hill Press, 1993), 64.

[4]Mary Schoesser and Celia Rufey, *English and American Textiles from 1790 to the Present* (New York: Thames and Hudson, Ltd., 1989), 245, note 49.

[5]*Washburn & Co.'s Amateur Cultivator's Guide to the Flower and Kitchen Garden . . .* (Boston: Washburn and Company, 1868), 8–10; G. M. Kern, *Practical Landscape Gardening . . .* (Cincinnati: Moore, Wilstach, Keys & Co., 1855), 211–215; *Godey's Lady's Book* 45 (July 1852), 82; A. J. Downing, *Cottage Residences; Or, a Series of Designs for Rural Cottages and Cottage Villas, and their Gardens and Grounds Adapted to North America* (New York, John Wiley, 1853), 188–199.

6Mrs. Loudon, *Gardening for Ladies, and Ladies' Companion to the Flower Garden*, ed. A. J. Downing (New York: Wiley and Putnam, 1843), Introduction; John T. C. Clark, *The Amateurs' Guide and Flower-Garden Directory* (Washington: 1856); Henry W. Cleaveland, William Backus, and Samuel D. Backus, *The Requirements of American Village Homes* . . . (reprint, New York: Appleton, 1856).

7*Godey's Lady's Book* 58 (1859), 562; *The Lorain County (Ohio) News*, 24 October 1860, 16 October 1861, 28 May 1862, 14 October 1863.

8Elizabeth B. Keeney, *The Botanizers: Amateur Scientists in Nineteenth-Century America* (Chapel Hill: University of North Carolina Press, 1992).

9Keeney, *Botanizers*, 41, 69, 70.

10Janet Gray Crosson, *Let's Get Technical: An Overview of Handwoven Pennsylvania Jacquard Coverlets: 1850–1860* (Lancaster, Pennsylvania: Old Fibers, Weavers, & Coverlets, 1978), 23.

11Rabbit Goody, "James Alexander Coverlets"; Clarita Anderson and Steven M. Spivak, "Some Preliminary Thoughts on the Machinery Involved in Early Coverlet Weaving," in *Woven Coverlets: Textiles in the Folk Tradition*, ed. Patricia A. Cunningham (Bowling Green, Ohio: Bowling Green State University, 1984), 20–23.

12Crosson, *Let's Get Technical*, 25; Edgar de N. Mayhew and Minor Myers, Jr., *A Documentary History of American Interiors From the Colonial Era to 1915* (New York: Charles Scribner's Sons, 1980), plates 8, 10; Gail Caskey Winkler and Roger W. Moss, *Victorian Interior Decoration* (New York: Henry Holt and Company, 1986), plate 1; Elizabeth Donaghy Garrett, *At Home: The American Family 1750–1870* (New York: Harry N. Abrams, Inc., 1990), 54, 121.

13I am grateful to Virginia Gunn, who suggested this explanation.

14Virginia Churchill Bath, *Lace* (Chicago: Henry Regnery Company, 1974), 63–70.

15Rexford Newcomb, *Architecture of the Old Northwest Territory* 27, 65–137; Clifford E. Clark, Jr., "Domestic Architecture as an Index to Social History: The Romantic Revival and the Cult of Domesticity in America, 1840–1870," *Journal of Interdisciplinary History* 7:1 (Summer 1976), 35. Benjamin's guides include *The Country Builder's Assistant* (1797), *The American Builder's Companion* (1806 and following), *The Rudiments of Architecture* (1814 and following), *The Practical House Carpenter* (1830), *The Practice of Architecture* (1833), *The Builder's Guide* (1839), and *The Elements of Architecture* (1843). Lafever published *The Young Builder's General Instructor* (1829), *The Modern Builder's Guide* (1833 and following), *The Beauties of Modern Architecture* (1835), and *The Architectural Instructor* (1856). Both architects include measured drawings of authentic Greek structures.

16Elisabeth Donaghy Garrett, *At Home*, 163.

17Winkler and Moss, *Victorian Interior Decoration*, 66, 67.

18See especially Winkler and Moss, *Victorian Interior Decoration*; Mayhew and Myers, *Documentary History*. For English examples, see Caroline Davidson, *Women's Worlds: The Art and Life of Mary Ellen Best 1809–1891* (New York: Crown Publishers, Inc., 1985).

19Gunn, "Victorian Silk Template Patchwork in American Periodicals 1850–1875," *Uncoverings 1985*, 9–25; *Godey's Lady's Book* 45 (July 1852), 4; 44 (March 1852), 184; John Tebbel and Mary Ellen Zuckerman, *The Magazine in America 1741–1990* (New York: Oxford University Press, 1991), 33.

20Clark et al., *Quilts in Community*, 20–30, 81–84; Barbara Brackman, Jennie A. Chinn, Gayle R. Davis, Terry Thompson, Sara Reimer Farley, and Nancy Hornback, *Kansas Quilts & Quilters* (Lawrence: University Press of Kansas, 1993), 67–91.

21Scott T. Swank et al., *Arts of the Pennsylvania Germans* (New York: W. W. Norton & Company, 1983); Stanley A. Kaufman with Ricky Clark, *Germanic Folk Culture in Eastern Ohio* (Walnut Creek, Ohio: German Culture Museum), 1986; Ellen J. Gehret et al., *This Is the Way I Pass My Time* (Birdsboro, Pennsylvania: The Pennsylvania German Society, 1985).

22Marcia MacDonald, "Handwoven Coverlets: Wayne County, Ohio, 1830–1860" (Art History Independent Study, The College of Wooster, 1976–1977), 82–89.

23Clark et al., *Quilts in Community*, 45; Nancy Hornback, *Quilts in Red and Green: The Flowering of Folk Design in 19th Century America* (Wichita, Kansas: Wichita/Sedgwick County Historical Museum,

1992), 4; Patricia A. Cunningham, "Ohio's Woven Coverlets: Textile Industry in a Rural Economy," *Ars Textrina*, vol. 2 (1984), 166.

Spreading the Word: Dissemination of Style and Patterns

[1]Virginia Gunn, "Victorian Silk Template Patchwork," 9–25.
[2]Ramsey, "Roses," 12–14.
[3]*Lorain County News*, 16 October 1861; *Elyria Independent Democrat*, 20 October 1858.
[4]Percy Wells Bidwell and John I. Falconer, *History of Agriculture in the Northern United States 1620–1860* (Washington: Carnegie Institution of Washington, 1925), 317–318; Albert Lowther Demaree, *The American Agricultural Press 1819–1860* (New York: Columbia University Press, 1941), 197–230.
[5]Wayne Caldwell Neely, *The Agricultural Fair* (New York: Columbia University Press, 1935), 84, 86; Donald B. Marti, *Historical Directory of American Agricultural Fairs* (New York: Greenwood Press, 1986), 120, 130, 163; A. T. Andreas, *History of the State of Nebraska . . .* (Chicago: Western Historical Company, 1882), 220.
[6]Robert Leslie Jones, *History of Agriculture in Ohio to 1880* (Kent, Ohio: Kent State University Press, 1983), 291; *Jeffersonian Democrat*, 24 September 1856; the census of 1850; Kenyon L. Butterfield, "Farmers' Social Organizations," vol. 4 of *Cyclopedia of American Agriculture*, ed. L. H. Bailey (New York: Macmillan Co., 1912), 291.
[7]"Independent Societies," *19th Annual Report of the Ohio State Board of Agriculture for 1864* (hereafter *AROSBA for 18—*), 3.
[8]"Report of the Ashtabula County Agricultural Society," "Report of the Lorain County Agricultural Society," *15th AROSBA for 1860*, 3, 42; (Cleveland) *Plain Dealer*, 10 October 1870 and 16 September 1871; "Report of the Montgomery County Agricultural Society," *30th AROSBA for 1875*, 267; "Report of the Wood County Agricultural Society," *32nd AROSBA for 1877*, 218.
[9]*6th AROSBA for 1851*, 18; *11th AROSBA for 1856*, 157; *5th AROSBA for 1850*.
[10]"Clermont County," *20th AROSBA for 1865*; *Medina Gazette*, 13 October 1858; Jones, *Agriculture*, 291.

[11]"Cuyahoga County," *24th AROSBA for 1869*; "State Fairs," *11th AROSBA for 1856*.
[12]*Painesville Telegraph*, 7 September 1865; "The County Fair," *The Lorain Argus* (Elyria, Ohio), 4 October 1854.
[13]*Lorain County News*, 23 May 1860, 28 May 1862, 14 October 1863, 12 October 1864; *Scioto Gazette*, 6 October 1847.
[14]*19th AROSBA for 1864*, 90.
[15]*Ashtabula Sentinel*, 16 October 1856; *Painesville Telegraph*, 5 October 1865–21 September 1871; *20th AROSBA for 1865–31st AROSBA for 1876*.
[16]"Fairfield County," *29th AROSBA for 1874*, 270.
[17]"Report of the Tuscarawas County Agricultural Society," *10th AROSBA for 1855*, 214.
[18]Virginia Gunn, "Quilts at Nineteenth Century State and County Fairs: An Ohio Study," *Uncoverings 1988*, 108.
[19]Hubert G. H. Wilhelm, *The Origin and Distribution of Settlement Groups: Ohio: 1850* (Athens, Ohio: by the author, 1982), 12.
[20]Craig Miner, *West of Wichita: Settling the High Plains of Kansas, 1865–1890* (Lawrence: University Press of Kansas, 1986), 38.
[21]Brackman et al., *Kansas Quilts & Quilters*, 87.
[22]"The Original Diary of Mrs. Laura (Downs) Clark, of Wakeman, Ohio," *Firelands Pioneer*, n.s.v. 21 (1920), 2308–2326; Eliza Farnham, *Life in Prairie Land* (New York: Harper & Brothers, 1846), 60–63.
[23]*Godey's Lady's Book*, April 1853; Louis Filler, ed., *An Ohio Schoolmistress*, 70.
[24]*17th AROSBA for 1862*, 109.

Conclusion

[1]Barbara Brackman et al., *Kansas Quilts & Quilters*, 13.
[2]One notable exception is the Hearts and Flowers quilt made by Lydia Melinda Blake, published in Clark et al., *Quilts in Community*, 127.
[3]John Michael Vlach, "The Concept of Community and Folklife Study" in *American Material Culture and Folklife: A Prologue and Dialogue*, ed. Simon J. Bronner (Ann Arbor: University of Michigan Research Press, 1985), 67.

Suggested Readings

Allen, Gloria Seaman. *First Flowerings: Early Virginia Quilts*. Washington, DC: DAR Museum, 1987.

———. *Old Line Traditions: Maryland Women and Their Quilts*. Washington, DC: DAR Museum, 1985.

Atkins, Jacqueline, and Phyllis A. Tepper. *New York Beauties: Quilts from the Empire State*. New York: Dutton Studio Books, 1992.

Bidwell, Percy Wells, and John I. Falconer. *History of Agriculture in the Northern United States 1620–1860*. Washington, DC: Carnegie Institution of Washington, 1925.

Bird, Michael, and Terry Kobayashi. *A Splendid Harvest: Germanic Folk and Decorative Arts in Canada*. Toronto: Van Nostrand Reinhold, Ltd., 1981.

Blum, Dilys, and Jack L. Lindsey. "Nineteenth-Century Appliqué Quilts." *Philadelphia Museum of Art Bulletin* 85 (Fall 1989).

Brackman, Barbara. "Fairs and Expositions: Their Influence on Quilts." In *Bits and Pieces: Textile Traditions*. Edited by Jeannette Lasansky, 90–95. Lewisburg, PA: Oral Traditions Project, 1991.

———. "Quiltmaking on the Overland Trail: Evidence from Women's Writings." *Uncoverings 1992*, 45–60.

Brackman, Barbara, Jennie A. Chinn, Gayle R. Davis, Terry Thompson, Sara Reimer Farley, and Nancy Hornback. *Kansas Quilts & Quilters*. Lawrence: University Press of Kansas, 1993.

Bresenhan, Karoline, and Nancy Puentes. *Lone Stars: A Legacy of Texas Quilts, 1836–1936*. Austin: University of Texas Press, 1986.

Buley, R. Carlyle. *The Old Northwest: Pioneer Period 1815–1840*. Indianapolis: Indiana University Press, 1950.

Burke, Susan M., and Matthew H. Hill. *From Pennsylvania to Waterloo: Pennsylvania–German Folk Culture in Transition*. Kitchener, Ontario: Joseph Schneider Haus, 1991.

Burnham, Harold B., and Dorothy K. Burnham. *Keep Me Warm One Night*. Toronto: University of Toronto Press and Royal Ontario Museum, 1972.

Campen, Richard N. *Architecture of the Western Reserve 1800–1900*. Cleveland: The Press of Case Western Reserve University, 1971.

Christie, Archibald. *Pattern Design: An Introduction to the Study of Formal Ornament*. New York: Dover Publications, Inc., 1969.

Clark, Clifford E., Jr., "Domestic Architecture as an Index to Social History: The Romantic Revival and the Cult of Domesticity in America, 1840–1870." *Journal of Interdisciplinary History* 7:1 (Summer 1976): 34–56.

Clark, Ricky, "Quilted Gardens." *Timeline* 10:5 (September–October 1993): 2–13.

Clark, Ricky, George W. Knepper, and Ellice Ronsheim. *Quilts in Community: Ohio's Traditions*.

Nashville: Rutledge Hill Press, 1991.

Cleveland, Richard L., and Donna Bister. *Plain and Fancy: Vermont's People and Their Quilts as a Reflection of America*. San Francisco: The Quilt Digest Press, 1991.

Cott, Nancy F. *The Bonds of Womanhood: "Woman's Sphere" in New England, 1780–1835*. New Haven: Yale University Press, 1977.

Cross, Mary Bywater. *Treasures in the Trunk: Quilts of the Oregon Trail*. Nashville: Rutledge Hill Press, 1993.

Cunningham, Patricia A. "Ohio's Woven Coverlets: Textile Industry in a Rural Economy." *Ars Textrina*, vol. 2 (December 1984): 165–183.

———. "Northwest Ohio Coverlet Weavers: An Update." *Northwest Ohio Quarterly* 58:1 (Winter 1986): 20–24.

———. "The Woven Record: Nineteenth-Century Coverlets and Textile Industries in Northwest Ohio." *Northwest Ohio Quarterly* 56:2 (Spring 1984).

Cunningham, Patricia A., ed. *Woven Coverlets: Textiles in the Folk Tradition*. Bowling Green, Ohio: Bowling Green State University, 1984.

Davidson, Caroline. *Women's Worlds: The Art and Life of Mary Ellen Best 1809–1891*. New York: Crown Publishers, Inc., 1985.

Demaree, Albert Lowther. *The American Agricultural Press 1819–1860*. New York: Columbia University Press, 1941.

Eanes, Ellen Fickling, Erma Hughes Kirkpatrick, Sue Barker McCarter, Joyce Joines Newman, Ruth Haislip Roberson, and Kathlyn Fender Sullivan. *North Carolina Quilts*. Chapel Hill: University of North Carolina Press, 1988.

Elbert, E. Duane, and Rachel Kamm Elbert. *History from the Heart: Quilt Paths Across Illinois*. Nashville: Rutledge Hill Press, 1993.

Faragher, John Mack. *Women and Men on the Overland Trail*. New Haven: Yale University Press, 1979.

Ferrero, Pat, Elaine Hedges, and Julie Silber. *Hearts and Hands: The Influence of Women & Quilts on American Society*. San Francisco: The Quilt Digest Press, 1987.

Fischer, Christiana, ed. *Let Them Speak for Themselves: Women in the American West, 1849–1900*. New York: E. P. Dutton, 1979.

Frary, I. T. *Early Homes of Ohio*. Richmond, Virginia: Garrett and Massie, 1936.

Garrett, Elizabeth Donaghy. *At Home: The American Family 1750–1870*. New York: Harry N. Abrams, Inc., 1990.

Gehret, Ellen J., Tandy Hersh, Alan G. Keyser, and Frederick S. Weiser. *This Is the Way I Pass My Time*. Birdsboro, Pennsylvania: The Pennsylvania German Society, 1985.

Green, Harvey, with Mary-Ellen Perry. *The Light of the Home: An Intimate View of the Lives of Women in Victorian America*. New York: Pantheon Books, 1983.

Gunn, Virginia. "Quilts at Nineteenth Century State and County Fairs: An Ohio Study." *Uncoverings 1988*, 105–128.

———. "Victorian Silk Template Patchwork in American Periodicals, 1850–1875." *Uncoverings 1983*, 9–25.

Heisey, John W., and Gail Andrews. *A Checklist of American Coverlet Weavers*. Williamsburg, Virginia: Abby Aldrich Rockefeller Folk Art Center, 1978.

Heritage Quilt Project of New Jersey. *New Jersey Quilts 1777–1950: Contributions to an American Tradition*. Paducah, Kentucky: American Quilter's Society, 1992.

Higham, John. *From Boundlessness to Consolidation: The Transformation of American Culture 1848–1860*. Ann Arbor: William L. Clements Library, 1969.

Holbrook, Stewart A. *The Yankee Exodus: An Account of Migration from New England*. New York: The Macmillan Co., 1950.

Holstein, Jonathan. "The American Block Quilt." In *In the Heart of Pennsylvania Symposium Papers*. Edited by Jeannette Lasansky, 16–27. Lewisburg, Pennsylvania: Oral Traditions Project, 1986.

Hornback, Nancy. *Quilts in Red and Green: The Flowering of Folk Design in Nineteenth-Century America*. Wichita, Kansas: Wichita/Sedgwick County Historical Museum, 1992.

Horton, Laurel, and Lynn Robertson Myers. *Social Fabric: South Carolina's Traditional Quilts*. Columbia, South Carolina: McKissick Museum, n.d.

Indiana Quilt Registry Project, Inc. *Quilts of Indiana: Crossroads of Memories*. Bloomington: Indiana University Press, 1991.

Jeffrey, Julie Roy. *Frontier Women: The Trans-Mississippi West 1840–1880*. New York: Hill and Wang, 1979.

Jensen, Joan M., ed. *With These Hands: Women Working the Land*. Old Westbury, New York: Feminist Press, 1980.

Jones, Howard Mumford. *O Strange New World: American Culture: The Formative Years*. New York: Viking Press, [1964].

Jones, Robert Leslie. *History of Agriculture in Ohio to 1880*. Kent, Ohio: Kent State University Press, 1983.

Juster, Norton. *So Sweet to Labor: Rural Women in America 1865–1895*. New York: The Viking Press, 1979.

Katzenberg, Dena S. *Baltimore Album Quilts*. Baltimore: The Baltimore Museum of Art, 1981.

Kaufman, Stanley A., with Leroy Beachy. *Amish in Eastern Ohio*. Walnut Creek, Ohio: German Culture Museum, 1990.

Kaufman, Stanley A., with Ricky Clark. *Germanic Folk Culture in Eastern Ohio*. Walnut Creek, Ohio: German Culture Museum, 1986.

Kaufman, Stanley A., with Dr. Lawrence W. Hartzell. *Moravians in Ohio*. Walnut Creek, Ohio: German Culture Museum, 1987.

Keeney, Elizabeth B. *The Botanizers: Amateur Scientists in Nineteenth-Century America*. Chapel Hill: University of North Carolina Press, 1992.

Kentucky Quilt Project. *Kentucky Quilts 1800–1900*. Louisville: The Kentucky Quilt Project, 1982.

Kimball, Jeana. *Red and Green: An Appliqué Tradition*. Bothell, Washington: That Patchwork Place, 1990.

Kolodny, Annette. *The Land Before Her: Fantasy and Experience of the American Frontiers, 1630–1860*. Chapel Hill: University of North Carolina Press, 1984.

————. *The Lay of the Land: Metaphor as Experience and History in American Life and Letters*. Chapel Hill: University of North Carolina Press, 1975.

Lasansky, Jeannette. *In the Heart of Pennsylvania: 19th and 20th Century Quiltmaking Traditions*. Lewisburg, Pennsylvania: Oral Traditions Project, 1985.

————. *Pieced by Mother: Over 100 Years of Quiltmaking Traditions*. Lewisburg, Pennsylvania: Oral Traditions Project, 1987.

Lasansky, Jeannette, ed. *Bits and Pieces: Textile Traditions*. Lewisburg, Pennsylvania: Oral Traditions Project, 1991.

————. *In the Heart of Pennsylvania Symposium Papers*. Lewisburg, Pennsylvania: Oral Traditions Project, 1986.

Laurie, Jean Ray, and the California Heritage Quilt Project. *Ho for California! Pioneer Women and Their Quilts*. New York: E. P. Dutton, 1990.

Leighton, Ann. *American Gardens of the Nineteenth Century: "For Comfort and Affluence."* Amherst: University of Massachusetts Press, 1987.

MacDowell, Marsha, and Ruth D. Fitzgerald, eds. *Michigan Quilts: 150 Years of a Textile Tradition*. East Lansing: Michigan State University Museum, 1987.

Maines, Rachel. "Paradigms of Scarcity and Abundance: The Quilt as an Artifact of the Industrial Revolution." In *In The Heart of Pennsylvania Symposium Papers*. Edited by Jeannette Lasansky, 84–89. Lewisburg, Pennsylvania: Oral Traditions Project, 1986.

Marx, Leo. *The Machine in the Garden: Technology and the Pastoral Ideal in America*. New York: Oxford University Press, 1964.

Mayhew, Edgar de N., and Minor Myers, Jr. *A Documentary History of American Interiors from the Colonial Era to 1915*. New York: Charles Scribner's Sons, 1980.

McCauley, Daniel, and Kathryn McCauley. *Decorative Arts of the Amish of Lancaster County*. Intercourse, Pennsylvania: Good Books, 1988.

Miner, Craig. *West of Wichita: Settling the High Plains of Kansas, 1865–1890*. Lawrence: University Press of Kansas, 1986.

Myres, Sandra. *Westering Women and the Frontier Experience 1800–1915*. Albuquerque: University of New Mexico Press, 1982.

Nash, Roderick. *Wilderness and the American Mind*. New Haven: Yale University Press, 1967.

Neely, Wayne Caldwell. *The Agricultural Fair*. New York: Columbia University Press, 1935.

Newcomb, Rexford. *Architecture of the Old Northwest Territory*. Chicago: University of Chicago Press, 1950.

Peesch, Reinhard, *The Ornament in European Folk Art*. Translated by Ruth Michaelis-Jena and Patrick Murray. New York: Alpine Fine Arts Collection, Ltd., 1982.

Prown, Jules David. "Style as Evidence." *Winterthur Portfolio* 15:3 (Autumn 1980): 197–210.

Ramsey, Bets. "Roses Real and Imaginary: Nineteenth-Century Botanical Quilts of the Mid-South." *Uncoverings 1986*, 9–25.

Ramsey, Bets, and Merikay Waldvogel. *Quilts of Tennessee: Images of Domestic Life Prior to 1930*. Nashville: Rutledge Hill Press, 1986.

Roan, Nancy, and Donald Roan. *Lest I Shall Be Forgotten: Anecdotes and Traditions of Quilts*. Green Lane, Pennsylvania: Goschenhoppen Historians, Inc., 1993.

Robertson, James Oliver. *American Myth, American Reality*. New York: Hill & Wang, 1980.

Sanford, Charles L. *The Quest for Paradise: Europe and the American Moral Imagination*. Urbana, Illinois: University of Illinois Press, 1961.

Schiffer, Margaret B. *Historical Needlework of Pennsylvania*. New York: Charles Scribner's Sons, 1968.

Schlissel, Lillian. *Women's Diaries of the Westward Journey*. New York: Schocken Books, 1982.

Schlissel, Lillian, Byrd Gibbens, and Elizabeth Hampsten. *Far from Home: Families of the Westward Journey*. New York: Schocken Books, 1989.

Schoesser, Mary, and Celia Rufey. *English and American Textiles from 1790 to the Present*. New York: Thames and Hudson, Ltd., 1989.

Schorsch, Anita. *Plain & Fancy: Country Quilts of the Pennsylvania-Germans*. New York: Sterling Publishing Co., Inc., 1992.

Smith, Henry Nash. *Virgin Land: The American West as Symbol and Myth*. Cambridge: Harvard University Press, 1950.

Speltz, Alexander. *Styles of Ornament Exhibited in Designs and Arranged in Historical Order with Descriptive Text*. Translated by David O'Conor. Berlin: Bruno Hessling, [1906].

Stith, Bari Oyler. "Visions of Community: Rural Culture in Nineteenth Century Geauga and Lake Counties." Ph.D. diss., Case Western Reserve University, 1992.

Stratton, Joanna L. *Pioneer Women: Voices from the Kansas Frontier*. New York: Simon and Schuster, 1981.

Sullivan, Kathy. "The Legacy of German Quiltmaking in North Carolina." In *Bits and Pieces: Textile Traditions*. Edited by Jeannette Lasansky, 64–71. Lewisburg, Pennsylvania: Oral Traditions Project, 1991.

Swank, Scott T., Benno M. Forman, Frank H. Sommer, Arlene Palmer Schwind, Frederick S. Weiser, Donald H. Fennimore, and Susan Burrows Swan. *Arts of the Pennsylvania Germans*. New York: W. W. Norton & Company, 1983.

Twelker, Nancyann Johanson. *Women and Their Quilts*. Bothell, Washington: That Patchwork Place, 1988.

Uncoverings. Sally Garoutte, ed. 1980–1986; Laurel

Horton, ed. 1987–1993; Virginia Gunn, ed. 1994– . Mill Valley and San Francisco, California: American Quilt Study Group.

Walker, Sandra Rambo. *Country Cloth to Coverlets: Textile Traditions* in *19th Century Central Pennsylvania*. Lewisburg, Pennsylvania: Oral Traditions Project, 1981.

Welter, Barbara. "The Cult of True Womanhood: 1820–1860." *American Quarterly* 18:2 (1966), 151–174.

Williams, Charlotte Allen. *Florida Quilts*. Gainesville: University Press of Florida, 1992.

Winkler, Gail Caskey, and Roger W. Moss. *Victorian Interior Decoration: American Interiors 1830–1900*. New York: Henry Holt and Company, 1986.

Index